PENGUIN BOOKS

# MARGARET MEAD

Phyllis Grosskurth is Profe[...] Toronto. She has edited The [...] has written biographies of Sy[...]nie Klein. Her reviews and articles [...] on both sides of the Atlantic.

## LIVES OF MODERN WOMEN

*General Editor: Emma Tennant*

Lives of Modern Women is a series of short biographical portraits by distinguished writers of significant twentieth-century women whose lives, ideas, struggles and creative talents contributed something new to a world in transition.

It is hoped that both the fascination of comparing the aims, ideals, set-backs and achievements of our grandmothers' generations with our own and the high quality of writing and insight will encourage the reader to delve further into the lives and work of those who have helped carve out a more acceptable and challenging place in society for the women of today.

*Titles already published in this series*

Hannah Arendt — Derwent May

Simone de Beauvoir — Lisa Appignanesi

Annie Besant — Rosemary Dinnage

Elizabeth Bowen — Patricia Craig

Vera Brittain — Hilary Bailey

Colette — Allan Massie

Sylvia and Christabel Pankhurst — Barbara Castle

Jean Rhys — Carole Angier

Bessie Smith — Elaine Feinstein

Freya Stark — Caroline Moorehead

Mme Sun Yat-sen — Jung Chang with Jon Halliday

Rebecca West — Fay Weldon

Phyllis Grosskurth

# Margaret Mead

Penguin Books

For Anne

PENGUIN BOOKS

Published by the Penguin Group
27 Wrights Lane, London W8 5TZ, England
Viking Penguin Inc., 40 West 23rd Street, New York, New York 10010, USA
Penguin Books Australia Ltd, Ringwood, Victoria, Australia
Penguin Books Canada Ltd, 2801 John Street, Markham, Ontario, Canada L3R 1B4
Penguin Books (NZ) Ltd, 182–190 Wairau Road, Auckland 10, New Zealand

Penguin Books Ltd, Registered Offices: Harmondsworth, Middlesex, England

First published 1988

Photographs are reproduced by permission of The Library of Congress,
Washington DC, USA

Made and printed in Great Britain by
Richard Clay Ltd, Bungay, Suffolk
Typeset in Monophoto Photina

# CONTENTS

## LIST OF PLATES

| | |
|---|---|
| 1901 | Birth of Margaret Mead, 16 December |
| 1919 | Enters De Pauw University |
| 1920 | Enters Barnard |
| 1923 | Marries Luther Cressman |
| 1925–6 | Field trip to Samoa |
| 1927 | Joins staff at the American Museum of Natural History |
| 1928 | Publication of *Coming of Age in Samoa*<br>Marries Reo Fortune |
| 1929 | Field trip to Manus |
| 1930 | Field trip to Nebraska |
| 1931–2 | Field trip to New Guinea |
| 1936 | Marries Gregory Bateson |
| 1936–7 | Field trip to Bali |
| 1939 | Birth of Mary Catherine Bateson, 8 December |
| 1942–5 | War work for National Research Council's Committee on Food Habits |
| 1950 | Divorce from Gregory Bateson |
| 1953 | Return to Manus |
| 1969 | Birth of granddaughter, Vanni Kassarjian |
| 1953–73 | Field trips to New Guinea, Bali, Montserrat |
| 1978 | Death of Margaret Mead, 15 November |

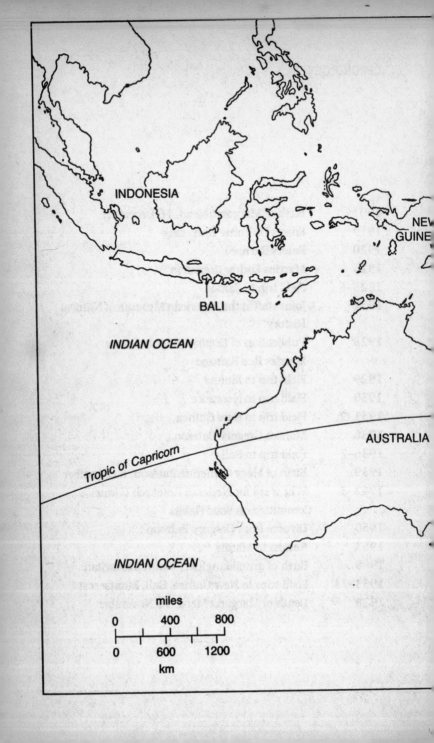

Area of Margaret Mead's
field trips, 1925–73

Samoa
Manus
Bali
New Guinea

*PACIFIC OCEAN*

US

*PACIFIC OCEAN*

SAMOA ▪

TASMANIA

NEW ZEALAND

# MARGARET MEAD

## CHAPTER ONE

## The Punk

Margaret Mead was as American as apple pie. She believed in efficient know-how. She believed that the world could be made a better place. She believed that there were answers to everything – and she knew a lot of them. Such confidence would inevitably inspire both adoration and disgruntlement.

Her background provided a fertile ground for her convictions. Born on 16 December 1901 to a family of agnostic educators, she learned early that a day was wasted if one did not learn something and, ideally, impart that knowledge to others. Her father, an economist in the Wharton School of Commerce at the University of Pennsylvania, taught her to fuse theory and practice. Her mother, who had majored in sociology at Wellesley College, was an early feminist who was more concerned about causes than about comfort and more interested in the vegetable garden than in flowers. From the numerous committees organized by Emily Fogg Mead, Margaret learned how to utilize the potential of individuals within a group.

It was a family not given to demonstrations of affection. Edward Mead addressed his small daughter as 'Punk', and when a brother was born when Margaret was two, Richard became known as 'the boy Punk', a secondary position which pleased Margaret although she always resented that he was obviously their father's favourite. Margaret's 'transitional object', a blanket, was her essential comforter. In later life it was replaced by a small pillow which she took on all her travels. A second daughter, Katherine, died in infancy when Margaret was four. Then two more girls came along, sisters who formed almost a second family. Margaret was always somewhat distant from them, critical of the beautiful Priscilla's 'shallowness' and impatient with Elizabeth's volatility.

The greatest influence on her childhood was her paternal grandmother, Martha Mead, who had moved in with the family shortly after her parents' marriage. From her Margaret learned algebra and was encouraged to make notes on how the vocabulary of her young sisters developed, just as Emily Mead had filled notebooks with observations on Margaret when she was little. Margaret was more hurt than she ever acknowledged when Elizabeth replaced her as Grandma's confidante. In later life she said that she was writing for her grandmother as 'the centre of my audience', and she was aware always that she had to convince her that she had made a wise decision in becoming an anthropologist. The trouble with Margaret was the fact that she took pains to give the impression that she didn't need anyone, while everyone needed her. 'I am just the catalytic agent which precipitates a large number of irrational loyalties, to the peace and well being of all of you I trust,' she once loftily informed her mother after she had moved away from home.

The family moved frequently, as Edward Mead went from place to place establishing branches of the University. They stayed in Philadelphia in the winter and occupied as many as three other houses during the rest of the year. In these moves Margaret assumed managerial responsibility by organizing each new household, choosing the most private room for herself, and staking out the 'pattern' of the local terrain. At the schools she attended fitfully, she would survey the group initially to ascertain who was friend or foe.

Although much time was spent in the country, the family did not evince any interest in the beauties of nature. Nor was it a family in which there was much laughter or games unless they were organized affairs. Perhaps the over-zealous atmosphere of his home tempted Edward Mead's eye to stray, and even as a girl Margaret was aware that her father was given to romantic affairs. There was one particularly serious one with a redhead which was quashed by his strong-minded mother, but his wife continued to make bitter remarks about it from time to time.

The Meads had unorthodox ideas about education. They disapproved of most schools, and the children were sent to various specialized instructors. Emily Mead encouraged her eldest daughter's interest in painting, securing as a teacher the most gifted person in the community in which they had temporarily alighted. However, Margaret abandoned the ambition of painter for that of writer around the time she went to college. With her erratic education, she had time to write novels and keep extensive diaries.

In her teens Margaret accompanied her serious mother on a fact-finding investigation of the effects of language on

IQ scores among Italian immigrant children, a project that she was to utilize in her master's dissertation in her final year at Barnard. Margaret had set her heart on following her mother to Wellesley, but her father had suffered financial losses from investments and in 1919 she had to settle for his university of De Pauw in Gruncastle, Indiana. Here she was a total misfit. Her Eastern accent sounded funny in the mid-West, her clothes were ludicrously old-fashioned, and she experienced the loneliness of being an outsider when she was not elected to a sorority to which all the 'worthwhile girls', as she put it, belonged. Her letters to her family were extraordinarily brave, and she choked back the tears when her classmates rejoined their families at Thanksgiving. However, when it seemed impossible to find money to pay for her fare to Philadelphia at Christmas, misery broke into her pleas. She admitted that it would be a 'moral defeat' to abandon De Pauw, but please, please, couldn't she come home for Christmas? She was rapturous with joy when somehow it was managed that she could be reunited with her family after all.

Before leaving for Indiana she had become engaged to Luther Cressman, a classics scholar who was destined for the ministry. At this point in life her aim was to be a minister's wife and the mother of a large family. It connoted respectability and service. And Luther seemed the ideal mate for her. She assured her mother, 'I am quite properly convinced that Luther is the most wonderful thing that ever happened or could happen to me.' At eleven Margaret had informed her astonished parents that she was going to be confirmed in the Episcopalian Church. Her bemused father grimly drove the determined adolescent to the service. When it became possible for her to transfer to Barnard College in 1920 after her one miserable year at De Pauw, she was able to persuade her fiancé to abandon his Lutheran faith and enrol in the General Theological Seminary in New York. Margaret Mead always had remarkable powers of persuasion.

At Barnard she blossomed in an all-female atmosphere. This time she was determined 'to belong'. She joined – or 'created', as she later put it – a group known as the 'Ash Can Cats'. These young women, living together in a series of apartments, established fierce loyalties which survived throughout their lives. 'Never break a date with a girl for a man' was one of their most sacred mottoes. The talents of one of them, the poet Léonie Adams, convinced Margaret that her own future lay not in literature but in other fields. Léonie's work forced her to acknowledge that her own poetry was rather derivative stuff, although she continued to write it, particularly during the first intensity of her relationship with Ruth Benedict.

Photographs taken at the time reveal a frankly plain, bespectacled girl. They do not convey her vivacity or her enthusiasm or her mop of blonde curls of which she was tremendously proud. Luther adored her. To be engaged was security for Margaret, because she knew that she didn't have to compete with other girls. After she became famous (and divorced from Luther) few people knew about his existence. In later life when she finally acknowledged publicly what she described as her 'student husband', Luther felt aggrieved that he had been regarded merely as a convenience at a stage when she feared that she couldn't get boyfriends.

The comradeship of the Ash Can Cats provided her with a sense of belonging which she had never known in her family's itinerant life. She invented a 'kinship' system for the group, with herself and Léonie Adams acting as parents. Demanding total devotion from her friends, she sulked all day in her room when they forgot her birthday. The Ash Can Cats taught her to play for the first time in her life, but it was infused with ritual, the only sort of play that really appealed to her. The most memorable event of her Barnard years was when the group presented the poet Edna St Vincent Millay with a May basket at midnight at the door of her Greenwich Village home. Margaret also discovered the delights of urban living, and years later could recall that she attended forty plays during her first semester. (Margaret's memory was crammed with precise figures for everything.)

Closely bonded as she was to these young women, Margaret's emotions were totally captivated by an anthropology instructor fifteen years her senior; and for the rest of her life Margaret was to retain her affection for Ruth Benedict. Benedict, lonely in a marriage which was soon to end, was touched by the devotion of her young friend and delighted by her eagerness to learn. She had first noticed her talking animatedly in a subway train. Hard of hearing, prone to stammer, Benedict always wore the same drab dress and her hair never stayed quite pinned up. Her beauty, which was to become legendary in later years, was in eclipse when Margaret first encountered her.

'I was the child she never had,' Margaret later recalled. 'I had all the things she wanted in a child: joy of living, positive affirmation of life – I worried that she'd lose interest in me because of the age discrepancy.' But what the painfully shy, withdrawn woman found enduringly attractive about Margaret was both her vitality and her comfort, which she compared to a chair into which one could snuggle. Margaret in turn adored the willowy woman with her soulful eyes and prematurely grey hair. While other students objected to the vague romanticism of her classes, Margaret was attracted to her deafness and her air of abstracted vulnerability.

It was Benedict who persuaded Margaret to become an anthropologist. She impressed her with the importance of doing field work, the urgency of recording the last traces of various cultures that were being obliterated. It was important to know about kinship systems, about the origins of traditions and values, and how a particular culture works and how it satisfies human needs. Benedict was the teaching assistant of the most eminent and controversial anthropologist of his time, Franz Boas. Before coming to Columbia Boas had taught at Clark University, which had bestowed an honorary degree on Freud in 1909. Boas had come into conflict with the university's president, G. Stanley Hall, both over Hall's espousal of psychoanalysis and over his belief that adolescence was a period of *Sturm und Drang* whereas Boas insisted that it was culturally determined. Boas had also been criticized for his pacifist stand during World War I.

Margaret became fascinated by this man, with his fierce moustache and the exotic sabre-cut on his cheek. Here was the mentor she had always been looking for. She had been majoring in psychology but was becoming increasingly excited by Boas's new ideas. They could be described as a reflection of the optimism rampant in America in the decade after the war, when the storm clouds of the Depression were not yet visible on the horizon. A whole new field of study – 'acculturation', the process whereby the members of one group adopt the customs of another – was the topic of the day. While there was emancipated talk about sex among the Ash Can Cats, Margaret learned that anthropologists were shocked by Freud's *Totem and Taboo* (English translation 1918 [1912–13]) in which he equated primitive man with the neurotic and the child.

Far more acceptable to the anthropological community were the pioneering behaviouristic theories of J. B. Watson. 'Behaviourism,' explained Watson, 'is the study of what people *do*.' Nurture, not nature, was responsible 'for what the child becomes'. Behaviour could be explained in purely cultural terms.

Margaret listened eagerly to Ruth Benedict's account of her work among the Plains Indians. Benedict's approach had been governed by Boas's historical diffusionist theory. Boas strongly objected to the theories of nineteenth-century unilinear evolutionists, who held that all cultures developed through an identical succession of stages. He rejected any single deterministic explanation of the origins or development of the world's cultures, a view that would leave a permanent stamp on Margaret's thinking.

Despite the ferment of ideas into which she had been plunged, Margaret adhered to her plan to marry Luther in 1923. Since they were both still graduate students her parents tried to persuade her to postpone the marriage; and her father even offered the inducement of a trip around the world. Luther himself was willing to wait until their lives seemed to be taking a more settled course. However, some demon of insecurity fired Margaret's determination. In a strange, half-humorous letter written to her mother on her honeymoon in Cape Cod, she informed her that she pitied her because she was not enjoying all the bridal excitements. Luther seemed to be very much of an afterthought.

And so he remained. Margaret insisted on retaining her maiden name, unusual at that time. 'I'm going to be famous some day,' she announced defiantly, 'and I'm going to be known by my own name!' They took an apartment in New York where they entertained frequently, but Luther always felt that he was being condescended to by Margaret's friends.

A decisive turning-point in Margaret's life occurred in 1924 when she attended a convention of the British Association for the Advancement of Science in Toronto. Here she gave a paper on Polynesian tattooing. It was her first taste of conferences, for which she immediately developed a lifelong addiction. Group adhesion and the flow of ideas within a structural framework was always immensely appealing to her.

On this occasion there was much discussion about Jung's *Psychological Types* (1923) and about Charles Seligman's suggestion that cultures might be thought of in psychiatric terms. Margaret had by now accepted that she had no specific talent, but she quickly grasped that anthropology was a field where intelligence and tenacity could be utilized. She was greatly impressed with the way these professionals talked possessively about *their* 'peoples'. She was determined to have a 'people' of her own, but it was not to be the American Indians, whom she considered had been studied to the point of tedium even by her beloved Ruth Benedict among the Zuñis in the Southwest States. What she wanted to work on was change, on the way new methods of doing things were related to tradition. Why not somewhere in Polynesia? What about Samoa?

At this point in the history of anthropology, English thought was dominated by A. R. Radcliffe-Brown (situated in Australia) and Bronislaw Malinowski, who emphasized functionalism, the study of the interdependence of the traits of a culture. In America Boas was insisting on the importance of field work in depth, with an understanding of the native language. The Americans concentrated on the American Indian, the English concentrated on the South Pacific and West Africa. Ultimately Margaret was to run into collision with Radcliffe-Brown for venturing into territory that had already been implicitly staked out.

Margaret also had 'Papa Franz', as Boas was affectionately known to his students, to contend with. Boas was extremely chivalrous to women in the field, concerned for their health and safety. Ruth went to bat for her protégée, convincing Boas that women could have access to certain areas of culture that were inaccessible to men. He eventually agreed to the project when he learned that a ship stopped at Pago Pago every three weeks.

The determining factor, however, was Boas's interest in adolescence, and he realized that Margaret might be able to provide original material on the degree to which the Samoan girl's behaviour is determined culturally and genetically. This would be far more important than stale findings from the over-examined Indians.

Edward Mead also finally capitulated and agreed to pay Margaret's fare. It was an act of faith on his part, considering that neither he nor his wife had ever been out of the United

States nor, for that matter, west of Iowa. It transpired that Luther's father had gone to college with the admiral in charge of the naval base at Samoa. And what was Luther to do while his wife was away? Margaret persuaded him of the advantages of taking a research scholarship in England. Luther always looked back to this exile as one of the most desperate periods in his life, but in Margaret's grand design there was an occasional human price to pay. Before her departure she took an ambitious trip, not with Luther but with Ruth Benedict, to the Grand Canyon, where they decided that they were more interested in each other than in the assorted males who were making importunate demands on them.

On the eve of Margaret's leavetaking in 1925 Boas wrote her a letter of advice. It was rather meagre in practicalities, particularly considering that she had not an inkling of what field work involved. To be fair, in anthropology it is difficult to specify what one should pay attention to in a society that has largely been undescribed. Boas expected students to learn their methodology from day-to-day contact. He emphasized that if she found that she couldn't stand the climate she should not feel ashamed to come home. As for the object of her expedition, 'the most important contribution that we hope you will make will be the psychological attitude of the individual under the pressure of the general pattern of culture'. This implied a certain set of assumptions upon which she should base her research. Yet years later she wrote of field work, 'To do it well, one has to sweep one's mind clear of every supposition.' In this same letter Boas stated that he believed that Malinowski had taken too 'Freudian an approach' (a passage Mead omitted from her autobiography,

*Blackberry Winter*). In other words, an ambitious young graduate student was being warned of the pitfalls to avoid. In 1928 she wrote to William Morrow that her research in Samoa had been 'an experiment to find out whether the difficulties of adolescent girls are due to physiological changes which take place at puberty or to the civilization in which they grow up'. A model had been established by Malinowski, who described the intimate details of the lives of the Trobriand Islanders in vivid profiles, although Margaret had read only one of his articles and, more importantly, was unfamiliar with the prior investigations of Samoa itself. The originality of her project was that no one had concentrated exclusively on women and children before.

The inexperienced innocent who started out on her great adventure in the summer of 1925 had never spent a day on her own. As she later looked back on the adventure, with some amusement she described herself as having 'all the courage of almost complete ignorance'. No one could ever accuse Margaret Mead of lacking guts.

Samoa comprises a group of islands in the South Pacific Ocean about 2,300 miles southwest of Hawaii. Traditionally it was divided into two parts after western traders arrived in the middle of the nineteenth century. Following World War I New Zealand administered Western Samoa as a League of Nations Mandate, while the United States governed eastern Samoa. As Margaret's ship sailed into Pago Pago on 31 August, planes roared overhead and a naval band played ragtime. The lush port fulfilled all her romantic dreams of the South Seas, imbibed from reading Robert Louis Stevenson.

However, the naval authorities who ran American Samoa

made it clear that they weren't too happy about being foisted with responsibility for a slip of a girl. Margaret, who had never stayed in a hotel in her life, spent six miserable weeks in the ramshackle hotel Somerset Maugham had made famous in *Rain*. Here she set about giving herself a quick course in the language – a difficult enterprise when she had never studied any language in depth – and the superficiality of her grasp of it was later to be a point of contention among her critics.

Field work, in which anthropologists live in a culture long enough to imbibe every aspect of its ethos, was just beginning when Mead entered the profession. Techniques, devised on the spot, were gradually absorbed into a system known as 'participant observation'. This involved often learning a language phonetically and adapting a system to record it,* learning how to trace and understand complicated relationships, and learning how to teach informers to be one's teachers. It was a process evolved from practical situations; and this little novice in her groping, earnest way did much to refine it. As Lola Romanucci-Ross has pointed out, from the beginning to the end of her career her methods were open-minded, excluding nothing that might add to her knowledge of a culture. Field work, as defined by Mead, was 'the intensive long months of trying to step as fully as one can into the reality of another culture'.

A half-Samoan woman, Mrs Wilson, who had been married to an American sailor and had lived in the United States, took Margaret under her wing. In some ways she was very helpful in giving her background information about Samoan

---

* Mead had available to her Pratt's *Grammar and Dictionary of the Samoan Language*, first published in 1862 with subsequent editions in 1876, 1892 and 1911.

customs; but it is possible that she was also an unfortunate influence if she filled her mind with some erroneous preconceptions.

In November Margaret arrived in Ta'ū, one of three small islands in the Manu'a group, about 70 miles east of Pago Pago. Ta'ū was chosen for three reasons: it was more primitive than any other part of Samoa; here she could find a cluster of adolescents; and she could board with an American family, the Holts, in the dispensary. To move in with the natives she rejected as impossible, because she found their food too starchy and she wanted some privacy. She was assailed by homesickness and longed for the monthly arrival of the steamer with its bundle of letters. Ruth's she read over and over. She did not reveal to anyone that she was married; and Luther, meanwhile, was becoming increasingly bitter that he had been shipped off to England solely, to his mind, for the convenience of Margaret's Samoan trip.

Margaret missed certain people, a bathtub, and a thick steak. The boredom and monotony of her routine was shattered a couple of months after her arrival by a devastating storm. She and the Holts emerged unscathed from the fury of the wind and the rain, but as the villagers determinedly went about rebuilding their demolished village, Margaret complained that 'it rather interferes with my work'.

The Holts gave her a verandah room at the back of the naval building, where she conducted daily interviews with twenty-five adolescent girls about their sexual lives. Although she was twenty-three, she looked about their age, as she weighed only ninety-eight pounds and was five feet two and a half inches tall. As a woman, she could not go anywhere alone and was not permitted to enter the ceremonial assemblies of chiefs. Her informants demanded gifts for their information, and within the first fortnight she had parted with masses of paper, cigarettes, matches, scissors, and other assorted items. She was debilitated by the heat and her head ached from the strain of listening. The sunset was the pleasantest time of the day, when everyone, she reported, waded into the sea. This seems to have been part of her romantic vision of Samoa. At night the villagers crowded into her room for dancing and incessant talk. Some Samoans later complained that she had stolen 'secrets' from them, but she asserted that no people had fewer secrets. Derek Freeman was to claim that the islanders had taken advantage of her gullibility. She was impressed by the way the girls moved from household to household and by their sense of ease within their society. In the few cases of deviant behaviour she encountered, as she saw it, the causes were patently explicable and often compounded by the expectations of the missionaries in their midst. (Freeman described these girls as actual delinquents.) Margaret's daughter, Mary Catherine Bateson, later realized that her mother was always looking for a single pervasive cultural configuration and that this expectation 'had led her to accept the limited view of their own culture given her by the young girls she worked with in Samoa, seeing Samoan culture as they did, as consistently moderate and serene, without seeking out the more aggressive cultural emphases of the young men'. To her publisher, William Morrow, Mead asserted categorically that 'the difficulties' of adolescent girls cannot be explained other than in terms of 'the social environment'. Clearly she had imbibed romantic notions about this tropical island, and perhaps she never returned to re-examine it lest her illusions be shattered.

Margaret spent nine months in all in Samoa. On the long voyage to Europe to rejoin Luther she rapidly fell in love with a handsome New Zealand psychologist, Reo Fortune, who was on his way to Cambridge with a two-year fellowship. Dark and intense, Fortune was also thirsting for companionship and the exchange of ideas. 'It was like meeting a stranger from another planet,' Margaret recalled, 'but a stranger with whom I had a great deal in common.' They discussed the work of W. H. R. Rivers, the Cambridge don who believed that man was motivated more by fear than by libido. Fortune also introduced her to Malinowski's *Argonauts of the Western Pacific*, which she had not yet read. Margaret was later to take a great dislike to the seasoned anthropologist when he declared publicly that nine months was too short a period in which to do any serious field work in Samoa.

Margaret met Luther at the dock in Marseilles with very uneasy feelings. She was the last passenger off the ship as she anguished with Reo as to whether she should accompany him to England. She subsequently confessed to Luther that she had fallen in love with someone else, but they nevertheless continued with their projected tour around France. Luther, meanwhile, had decided to leave the ministry and had accepted a teaching job in the sociology department at City College in New York. Reo turned up in Paris; and Luther could be in no doubt about the relationship when he discovered Margaret and Reo locked in each other's arms when he returned one day to their hotel room. However, he found the situation less than intolerable since he had already met an English woman whom he was later to marry. Before leaving Europe, Margaret had a pre-arranged reunion with Ruth Benedict in Rome where they attended a conference together.

For the time being Margaret decided to continue living with Luther in New York. She basked in the exotic status and the fuss that was made over her, while Luther was relegated more than ever to the background. In *Blackberry Winter* she says frankly that she was hurt because many people thought that she was 'exploiting' him. At the American Museum of Natural History she was appointed an assistant curator, and was given an office in the sixth floor tower which was to be as much her home as any dwelling for the rest of her professional life. Her association with the Museum provided her with a background of prestige and flexibility. Founded in 1869, the Museum was famous not only for its mounted specimens of animals from all over the world but also for its active research in animal behaviour, anthropology, paleontology, and many other areas.

Margaret had changed – at least, she was gaining a sense of her own importance. She asserted her independence in an extraordinary letter to her mother, dated 20 December 1927. This was a dramatic contrast to the letters she had written from De Pauw begging to be allowed to come home for Christmas. Now she declared that she would return only on her own terms – namely, that her mother accept the fact that she regarded her family as impersonally as anyone to whom she was not related. As for anything her parents had done for her, she considered it of little value if it had been done simply because she was their daughter. Margaret was not always lovingly remembered for her unsolicited advice and compulsive meddling in other people's lives.

Nevertheless, she left it to her mother to break the news

to Mrs Cressman, Luther's mother, that the marriage was over, that she hadn't cared for Luther in the way that was right for marriage, and that it was just 'bad luck', etc. Life as the wife of a minister and the mother of six children was discarded with other youthful images. In June 1928 she travelled to Mexico to put in the two requisite months for a divorce. At that time, this tactic was favoured as being the simplest way to avoid the many complications of an American divorce. On her return to New York she threw herself into the excitement of the publication of *Coming of Age in Samoa*. She regarded her dissertation as of relative unimportance in comparison with the book. Before she left for Samoa she had completed 'An Inquiry into the Question of Cultural Stability in Polynesia',* which was a survey of what Mead called the 'complexei' of canoe-building, house-building and tattooing in Hawai, the Marquesas, Tahiti and Samoa.

Encouraged by Ruth Benedict, she had prepared a manuscript on her impressions of Samoan adolescents. Rejected first by Harper & Bros, it was accepted by William Morrow provided she focus on the way her findings had relevance for youth in America. Her entire career would be devoted to finding patterns, connections, and models which linked far-off places to her own culture, place, and time. She announced jubilantly to her mother that the whole staff at the Museum was taking a personal interest in the process of publication and that it was like 'having the first baby in a new hospital'. Later in her autobiography, *Blackberry Winter*, she recorded that Boas had given his laconic approval to the manuscript; and his only criticism was that she had not distinguished

* Not published until 1928.

clearly enough 'the difference between passionate and romantic love'. However, he provided a Foreword to the book in which he made clear his own bias:

In our own civilization the individual is beset with difficulties which we are likely to ascribe to fundamental human traits. When we speak about the difficulties of childhood and adolescence, we are thinking of them as unavoidable periods of adjustment through which everyone has to pass. The whole psychoanalytic approach is largely based on this supposition.

. . . up to this time hardly anyone has taken the pains to identify himself sufficiently with a primitive population to obtain an insight into these problems. We feel, therefore, grateful to Miss Mead for having undertaken to identify herself so completely with Samoan youth that she gives us a lucid and clear picture of the joys and difficulties encountered by the young individual in a culture so entirely different from our own. The results of her painstaking investigation confirm the suspicion long held by anthropologists, that much of what we ascribe to human nature is no more than a reaction to the restraints put upon us by our civilization.

Havelock Ellis was also persuaded to give it a glowing tribute, which was printed on a red band to encircle the book as a sales gimmick.

The book was hailed as a classic from the moment of its publication, although Margaret did not learn of the full extent of its success until many months later when she had returned to the South Pacific. There she received word that it had become a best-seller. Its great popular appeal lay in the fact that it said exactly what people wanted to hear in the most seductive of language. Here is its opening description of a day in Samoa.

The life of the day begins at dawn, or if the moon has shown until daylight, the shouts of the young men may be heard before dawn from the hillside. Uneasy in the night, populous with ghosts, they shout lustily to one another as they hasten with their work. As the dawn begins to fall among the soft brown roofs and the slender palm trees stand out against a colourless, gleaming sea, lovers slip home from trysts beneath the palm trees or in the shadow of beached canoes, that the light may find each sleeper in his appointed place. Crows crow, negligently, and a shrill-voiced bird cries from the breadfruit trees. The insistent roar of the reef seemed muted to an undertone for the sounds of a waking village. Babies cry, a few short wails before sleepy mothers give them the breast. Restless little children roll out of their sheets and wander drowsily down to the beach to freshen their faces in the sea. Boys, bent upon an early fishing, start collecting their tackle and go to rouse their more laggard companions. Fires are lit, here and there, the white smoke hardly visible against the paleness of the dawn. The whole village, sheeted and frowsy, stirs, rubs its eyes, and stumbles towards the beach.

Her chief critic, Derek Freeman, later complained that if she had taken the trouble to read the literature of earlier observers, she would have learned that the Samoans were not gentle, uncompetitive, and guilt-free, but driven by rivalry and rank, and that they suffered from *musu* which Mead described as an expression of 'unwillingness and intractability', whereas Freeman and others have found it to be a form of destructive rage, often leading to suicide, particularly in adolescence, a period which Mead described as 'the age of maximum ease' in Samoa.

Mead described her visit as 'the ideal method of science, the method of controlled experiment, through which all hypotheses may be submitted to an objective test' – a high claim that was to haunt her in later years. Finally, in her conclusion, she launched into a diatribe against the unnatural restraints of American life, asserting that one could learn true freedom from the relaxed mores of the Samoans.

Margaret had apparently imbibed some of that freedom herself. She and Reo were now in a position to work together on a project: to test Freud's theory that primitive children displayed the same thought processes as neurotics. Where she had concentrated on adolescents in Samoa, she now turned to even younger children. It may seem puzzling that she used Freud as a referent, but then perhaps he had been the implicit referent in Samoa. From an opposite perspective, the wealthy French psychoanalyst Marie Bonaparte had subsidized the expedition of Geza Roheim (a Hungarian psychoanalyst and anthropologist) to Western Australia in order to disprove Malinowski's denial of the universality of the Oedipus complex. Was Margaret now bent on disproving a single deterministic theory purportedly applicable to all cultures?

Out of the thousands of tiny communities in Melanesia, she and Reo had decided to concentrate on the Admiralty Islands. This small volcanic group lies just south of the equator and about 200 miles north of New Guinea. Here Reo planned to pursue his interest in primitive religion. It was an area where no modern ethnographic research had been done, 'a priceless laboratory', as Margaret called it, a culture that would inevitably vanish in time.

And so in the autumn of 1928 Margaret set off on her second expedition to the South Seas – and for her second marriage. After the loneliness of Samoa, she was determined never to be on her own again. A man was essential, a

35

practical resource, even if she didn't happen to be sexually attracted to him. 'A professional partnership with Reo,' as she later bluntly put it, 'made more sense than cooperation with Luther in his career of teaching sociology.' However, she realized that children by this man, who was subject to volatile moods and whose parents seemed to her to be alarmingly unstable, might be very unwise, a decision based on the eugenics she professed to despise. Before her departure she made a will leaving her most precious possessions to Ruth Benedict and another close friend, Marie Eichelberger.

She joined Reo on 8 October 1928 in Auckland, where he insisted that they be married on the spot so that he would be able to present his bride to his mentor, A. R. Radcliffe-Brown, when they arrived in Sydney. On Radcliffe-Brown's advice they narrowed down their area of research to the sea-dwelling Manus people of the north coast of New Guinea.

In 1928 the Mandated Territory of New Guinea was administered by Australia, which had taken over from Germany after the war. Margaret and Reo arrived first in Rabaul, the biggest town on New Britain Island, a pretty tropical place with wide streets that had been laid out by the Germans. All seemed relatively peaceful in this community in which the European residents lived in bungalows set high on stilts, each household with its complement of house boys. However, shortly before the arrival of the Fortunes there had been a general strike by the indentured workers who had been forced to capitulate by their masters, and resentment smouldered under the surface.

Reo and Margaret did not stay long in Rabaul as they were eager to start work in Manus, an island about 300 miles to the northwest. Since they did not know the language they needed an interpreter. A group of teenage boys who had been sent from Manus to school in Rabaul were produced. For some reason they chose Bonyalo, a short, stocky unresponsive lad whose education now set him off completely from the other natives. Years later Margaret recalled that she was fully aware that 'he did not want to go: he liked school, he was resentful of being taken away from his schoolmates, and only the promise that he would be returned to Rabaul when we left mollified him at all'. He helped them over their first weeks of learning Pidgin English (later termed Melanesian Pidgin or Neo-Melanesian); but as they became more proficient, 'we dispensed with him more and more, and he understood very little about the culture and treated every task with grudging lack of enthusiasm. He wore khaki shorts and sulked.' Not surprisingly, they never communicated again after they parted, although many years later Mead learned that he had become a leader among his own people, a fact that surprised her as she continued to consider him unredeemably stupid.

The Fortunes first stopped at the government station at Lorengau, which was within a day's journey from their destination. Its colonial community was right out of Somerset Maugham: a state of permanent hatred, envy and heavy drinking prevailed among the whites. They were eager to be on their way.

The arrival at Bonyalo's village of Peré was the stuff of romance. As they poled into the fishing-village they saw dome-shaped houses standing on piles among palm trees in the shallow lagoon. It was primitive Venice, in which the natives could move about only by canoe. Even tiny children knew how to paddle. Here began a six-month investigation which Margaret was to look back on as the happiest collaborative effort she ever shared with Reo.

Nevertheless, the natives did not know how to accept a white woman in their midst. She suffered intermittently from malaria during their entire stay. People were constantly demanding money and the construction of their house was a nightmare. Unlike the insular Papua New Guinea peoples, the Manus were sailors and keen traders, always ready to make a deal. Every event was treated in terms of economics. Reo was trusted because he was 'dominating, definite, and trustworthy in trade'. He made an enormous impression when he flew into a rage after Margaret broke her ankle because of local carelessness about a makeshift bridge. Margaret frequently congratulated herself on the wisdom of her marriage.

Like the villagers, they lived in a house with a thatched roof on piles on the edge of a tiny island. The interior was lined with cupboards for stores, but filled as it was by the constant presence of children, baskets and locked cedarwood boxes were hung from the ceiling. There were lots of fish and vegetables and Reo would occasionally shoot a wild duck. But there was no privacy, and with the houses clustered closely together there was the din of shouting from one dwelling to another.

Peri seemed a paradise for children. The forty youngsters in the village led easy-going, undisciplined lives, as their mothers left them to their own devices after infancy. They smoked incessantly. For Margaret the curious thing about them was that there seemed to be no connection between these relaxed children and the harsh, competitive adults they would become within their monolithic culture. These observations were to disturb some progressive educators who believed children to be infinitely malleable.

In *Growing Up in New Guinea* Mead used her experience to chastise psychoanalysts with their 'unwearied desire to subsume the whole of life under one rubric'. She frankly declared that her study had been inspired by Watson, 'based on the assumption that the child is so subject to environmental influences that the only way to arrive at any conception of original nature is to study it as modified by difficult environmental conditions'. She hoped that Americans would recognize themselves in the Manus, particularly in their failure to provide adequate role models for their children. Furthermore, they should be grateful to anthropologists, she asserted, for forsaking the amenities of civilized life and subjecting themselves to 'the inconvenience and unpleasantness of life among a people whose manners, methods of sanitation, and ways of thought, are completely alien to them'.

She had brought with her a large assortment of toys – such as a wooden snake made of joints – as a means of evoking response in the children. At the time she knew nothing specific about Rorschach inkblot tests but she devised some of her own. She learned to take notes as fast as people talked without looking at her pad, and she typed them up while in the field so that she could publish her findings as quickly as possible on her return to civilization. In Samoa she had got into the habit of dating every note, aware that one never knew in advance when a piece might form part of a general pattern. Most important of all, she carried with her 1,000 sheets of drawing paper – which she used up within a month, mainly because the children didn't automatically draw 'animistic' pictures as she had anticipated.

In August 1929 Margaret and Reo sailed from Sydney to Vancouver. Burdened with sixteen pieces of luggage, they wearily made their way across the continent to New York. Here domestic life didn't prove any easier than it had been with Luther. Reo didn't approve of Margaret doing housework, yet he didn't indicate any interest in tidying his perpetual litter of papers. Years later Margaret was to describe their problems as one of the 'penalties of cross-national marriages, even without any of the complications that have been introduced by the changing roles of men and women'. While Margaret viewed herself as extremely progressive, it never seemed to occur to her to try to establish a shared partnership within the marriage.

Reo was still in effect a graduate student, while Margaret at least had a position at the Museum of Natural History despite the fact that her salary was frozen at $2,500 for years following the crash of 1929.

Reo tended to get bogged down with the details of the manuscript on which he was working, whereas the conscientious Margaret had already begun to write her second book, *Growing Up in New Guinea*. While preparing it she sent a long descriptive letter to Malinowski in London, explaining that the sex material would prove very disappointing because 'sex is almost legislated out of existence by a rigid supernaturally enforced moral code'. Malinowski was extremely sceptical that sex was as absent from Manus as she claimed. 'If so,' he asked, 'what results does it produce on intellectual integrity and nervous stability? A distinct predilection for copulatory pastimes seems to me the natural thing, and if our maiden aunts, who worshipped Queen Victoria, the White Lily, affected a considerable detachment we, usually, had to pay the price of their bad temper, and pre-Freudian complexes, that is unless there was something wrong with their ovaries.' Serious Margaret, who failed to notice when her leg was being pulled, replied that the bad temper of the Manus could be attributed to their method of child-training and poor living conditions, all of which seemed to discourage sex. 'Their intellectual integrity,' she assured him, 'is of a high order.'

This letter was written from an Omaha reservation in Nebraska where Ruth Benedict had persuaded Reo to spend three months in the summer of 1930. According to a disgruntled Margaret, they were doomed to endure a few educational months 'among these most dilapidated American Indians from which our very souls recoil'. She could not summon up any interest in them because they had been subjected to the imposition of many cultures and lacked the 'functional' purity of Oceania. This 'tiresome summer' was a 'mere interlude'. To Benedict she wrote, 'Don't think I am a thankless wretch, please. And scold me if you think I still deserve it and am overestimating the difficulties . . . I feel as if I had no sense of values left when I try to evaluate this work.' She would never again allow anyone else to dictate her destination or field of study.

In the spring of 1931 Margaret experienced some real criticism of her work. A review in the *Saturday Review of Literature* claimed that her second book, *Growing Up in New Guinea*, lacked any real knowledge of the Manus kinship system. She postponed their projected field trip until she had finished a monograph on 'Kinship in the Admiralty Islands', which was so detailed that she felt confident she could put the controversy behind her.

There was one constant throughout Mead's field work: each culture was viewed as a data base for problem-solving. While her methods became more refined with experience, she was always preoccupied with finding an answer to a topical question of universal interest. In Samoa she had found an alternative to sexual repression. On the ambitious project she and Reo were about to embark upon in New Guinea, she was to find evidence to support the contention that society pays a high cost for stereotyping sex roles.

In September 1930 they returned to New Guinea, this time to the northwest mountain region. They decided to limit themselves to a circumscribed area of investigation among the people Reo and Margaret referred to as the Arapesh, a generic word used by the natives for their relatives. For the first time they encountered really difficult travelling conditions through the mountainous jungle. The villagers of Alitoa were astonished to see a party of 150 porters ascending their steep hillside, and especially by the sight of a white woman borne on a hammock because of a weak ankle. Here the Fortunes established themselves for the next six months, simply because their porters refused to take them any farther.

They did not find it a particularly challenging culture to study, although husband and wife were to differ radically in their interpretation of the people, whom Margaret was to describe as unusually gentle, whereas Reo was struck by their violent, aggressive streak. He also found them the most complicated people in his experience. It is possible that some of their own difficulties affected their observations. At first Margaret was cheerful that they had found an 'excellent place to study the genesis of gender consciousness' as she noticed that the baby girls were ornamented from birth, that they soon flirted, and that women had certain assigned chores. However, she was discouraged by the natives' sullen resistance to her attempts to extract information from them. In this isolated spot she was plunged into a deep, paralysing depression. In a letter to Malinowski Reo informed him that he and his wife found working together 'full of excellent short cuts', but complained that he had a very depressed woman on his hands. As Margaret later looked back on this period, she realized that she had had too much time to think on top of a mountain usually shrouded in mist.

By July of 1932 they were relieved to end their sojourn among the Arapesh. Their next field trip was determined in almost as haphazard a fashion. They had heard that there was rich human material to be studied in the area of the Sepik River, also in the northwest part of what is now Papua New Guinea. The mighty Sepik River, 1,126 kilometres in length, starts in the mountains and winds slowly down to the sea like a brown, coiling serpent. It often turns back on itself, leaving huge swampy expanses; and at the end of the rainy season great chunks of mud and vegetation are torn out of the riverbank to float off downstream as drifting islands. Margaret found it an altogether dreary vista.

The most accessible tribe on its banks appeared to be the Mundugumor, who could be reached only by water and who had not come under the influence of missionaries, the perpetual bane of anthropologists. However, the Fortunes were no happier than they had been with the Arapesh. The ferocious mosquitoes and the humid climate did not help their domestic relationship.

In *Sex and Temperament* Mead was to write that regardless of gender, the Mundugumor men and women were both expected to be 'violent, competitive, aggressively sexed, and ready to see and avenge insult, delighting in display, in action, in *fighting*'. Reo, on the other hand, was not particularly disturbed by their behaviour. Margaret complained that 'they struck some note in him that was thoroughly alien to me'. She loathed the Mundugumor, and seemed to resent them for not providing adequate material from which she could make generalizations. The natives were 'superficially agreeable' but one could not ignore their cannibalism, headhunting, incest, and habit of biting lice in half with their teeth. In a rather revealing letter penned just before their final departure Margaret described the people as 'charming in many ways'. They seemed to be postponing their quarrels until after the strange white people had left. 'It takes adepts in hypocrisy to be sufficiently self-conscious to think of what a front they present to a white man.' But how could she be convinced that the Mundugumor were more susceptible to observation than the Manus, 'who are too sincere, or the Arapesh, who were too simple-minded'?

It was not uncommon to see unwanted babies floating down the stream. Margaret herself had begun to long for a baby, but she realized that Reo was not at all the sort of man she would consider a suitable father. The marriage was doomed to failure when after seven and a half months of incarceration they set off for Ambunti, the government station on the Sepik, to join the other whites in the region for Christmas festivities – which mainly consisted of heavy drinking.

Margaret had heard much about an Englishman called Gregory Bateson who had been working among the Baining and Sulka people of New Britain and who was now investigating the Iatmul. On their fateful meeting their relationship was sealed when he remarked on how tired she looked, the first really kind words she had heard in months. A lanky man of six feet five inches, he towered protectively over the tiny American woman. Reo had known him slightly at Cambridge; and in his colonial truculence he regarded Bateson enviously as being able to make his way easily in the world through his established connections to the British intellectual aristocracy.

Bateson was the progeny of a distinguished line of academics. His father, William Bateson, was one of the founders of modern genetics. Bateson's first field work had been done among the Iatmul of New Guinea, investigations which led to his classic book, *Naven* (1936). After the loneliness and tension of the past months, the ill-assorted trio plunged into an orgy of talk. One night Reo woke to hear Margaret and Bateson in intense conversation. 'There is much to be said,' Mead observed perceptively in *Blackberry Winter*, 'for the suggestion that the true oedipal situation is not the primal scene but parents talking to each other in words the child does not understand. And by then Gregory and I had established a kind of communication in which Reo did not share.'

The Fortunes, under Bateson's influence, decided to study a people on the Aimbom Lake, 180 miles from the mouth of the Sepik. They called these lake people the Tchambuli, although they are now known to ethnographers as the Chambri. Margaret caught her breath at her first sight of the lake, covered with thousands of lotuses and water lilies, which inevitably inspired her lyrical, descriptive powers.

Bateson set up his encampment only a few miles away so that he could paddle back and forth to the Fortunes' field site. They spent hours of intense talk in the eight-foot-square mosquito room Margaret and Reo had built for themselves. The working conditions were the best they had encountered since Manus: a compact tribe of about 550 people from which they selected a group of reliable informants. Bateson was impressed by Margaret's 'enormous visual and auditory greed for data'. At first he was shocked by the bullying manner of his friends towards the natives, although he gradually assumed some of their methods in order to wrest information out of his informants.

This 'imperialist' method of grabbing natives by the collar had been established by Malinowski and absorbed by Fortune while studying in England. 'I was at first shocked,' Bateson confessed in a letter to his mother. 'They bully and chivvy their informants and *harry* them till they don't know whether they are on head or heels. But in the end I was converted and I am going to do some bullying too . . . And they *plan* their work while I very gingerly pick up what comes.' They all worked with a manic intensity as their relationship accelerated to the breaking-point.

Again Margaret was to find that human nature was infinitely malleable in a society in which the women played the dominant role. During this period the manuscript of Ruth Benedict's *Patterns of Culture* arrived. This book was to intensify the cross-fertilization of ideas that had already been established among them. The idea that had most impact on them was Benedict's contention that there were not only enormous differences between cultures but enormous differences in individuals within the same culture. This was to have a profound effect upon Bateson because of Margaret's enthusiasm for typologies. It led to his formulation of the concept of schismogenesis, that is, 'the notion that there are progressive changes in relationships either of persons or of groups, and that those progressions are, in a sense, creative, evolutionary ...' Social relationships oscillate during a period of change in which a process of intensification of role takes place.

Margaret had been attracted to Reo because of his 'difference' after the familiarity of Luther. Now the Englishness of Bateson seemed to her as excitingly different as any foreign tribe. At this point she tended to identify both herself and Bateson with the nurturing Arapesh and Fortune with the aggressive Mundugumor. For years Reo smouldered with resentment at Margaret's insinuation that he was an aggressive Mundugumor type while she and Bateson were 'maternal' in contrast. He would write her an angry letter about the 'messianic message' in *Sex and Temperament*, which he saw as a rationalization of her behaviour rather than as objective field work. He charged that Bateson and Margaret had used their theories to justify their own behaviour and to rationalize their conviction that they were both deviants within their respective cultures.

Margaret had been trained in behaviourist psychology, but now her conversations with Bateson led her to entertain the possibility that human beings might be 'innately different' at birth and reared to behave in certain acceptable ways by their society. While Bateson drew on biological analogues, Margaret at that time found herself attracted to Jung's division of humans into four basic character types. 'It was exciting,' she later recalled, 'to strip off the layers of culturally attributed expected behaviour and to feel that one knew at last who one was.' It was a view that helped her ultimately to accept her own bisexuality. Cultural attitudes of this time required her to be extremely discreet about her relationships with other women, relationships which had been a continuing thread in her sexual life from her days at Columbia.

Naturally it was galling to Reo to watch his wife and Bateson falling in love, although when the three of them returned to Australia in the spring of 1933, for the time being they went their separate ways – Reo to England by way of New Zealand to visit his family, Bateson to Cambridge, and Margaret to New York to her job at the Museum. On her return she participated in the Hanover Seminar of Human Relations organized by Lawrence Frank. This was the first interdisciplinary conference she had attended, and it undoubtedly affected the views in *Sex and Temperament* (to be published in 1935), which she began writing while in New Hampshire. Frank introduced her to people like Erik Erikson and Robert and Helen Lynd who were then working on their monumental study, *Middletown*. All of them were to remain lifelong friends.

In the summer of 1934 she met Bateson in Ireland where their relationship was cemented, and he rejoined her the following year in the United States (by which time she was divorced from Reo), where they made plans for a field trip to Bali.

Following the example of Ruth Benedict in *Patterns of Culture*, in *Sex and Temperament* Margaret devoted her last chapter to the role of the deviant in society. Feminists responded well to the book, which they saw as abandoning gender stereotypes, but fourteen years later they were dis-

Margaret Mead at eighteen months, 1902.

Margaret with her mother, Emily Fogg Mead, 1905.

Margaret and her brother, Richard Mead, 1911.

Margaret Mead with fiancé Luther Cressman in 1918.

*Above left:* Mead (centre) with the Ash Can Cats.

*Above right:* Margaret Mead at Barnard, 1922.

*Below:* Margaret Mead with her second husband, Reo Fortune, in Manus, 1929.

*Above left:* Franz Boas.

*Above right:* Mead and her third husband, Gregory Bateson, whom she married in Singapore in 1936.

*Below:* Mead and Bateson working together in the mosquito room, Tambunam, New Guinea, 1938.

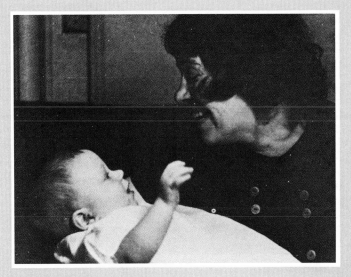

Margaret Mead with daughter Mary Catherine Bateson, 1940.

Mead on the lecture platform.          Ruth Benedict.

Margaret Mead at Delphi.

Grandmother to the world returns to Manus, 1953.

The participant-observer in the field.

Catherine Bateson, Barkev Kassarjian and their daughter Vanni.

Mead with her granddaughter Vanni,

turbed by the innate sexual differences she drew in *Male and Female*. Mead has always posited something of a problem to the women's movement. She competed on her own terms in a man's world, but she maintained certain traditional values about women. For example, she chastised Karen Horney because she believed that as 'one of the first prominent human scientists' she should have prevented schisms rather than initiating divisions within the psychoanalytic movement. She was also critical of Horney for what seemed her total lack of interest in children.

All Margaret's own relationships with men were doomed because of the dominating role she felt compelled to assume. Bateson described his fiancée to his possessive mother as 'small, very businesslike, and very quick intellectually . . . Is she a lady? Yes, if you will ever allow that term to an American.' He felt compelled to add that he believed she would find Margaret's family acceptable since they were 'rationalistic, agnostic, Spencer-reading New England Puritans'. As for Margaret's appearance, he described it unromantically as 'a good sound plain intelligent – almost female Darwin face'. He added that his chief feeling about their impending marriage was one of relief, particularly in knowing that he did not have to go into the field alone again.

According to Margaret's account in *Blackberry Winter*, Bateson had to finish the manuscript of *Naven* before he felt adequate to enter into an equal partnership. She, too, saw the professional advantages to the marriage. She had, as she confidently saw it, 'a lifetime of completed experience behind me', whereas Bateson's efforts to date had been incomplete and unsatisfying. Now they could pool their resources to produce something really fruitful.

49

Margaret was somewhat devious with her parents about her new relationship. Her mother might be emancipated intellectually – but how would she react to three marriages within ten years? After the wedding in Singapore on 13 March 1936, Margaret wrote home that this remarkable event had occurred after Bateson had pursued her to Java to persuade her to marry him. It was all, as she explained it, sudden and surprising.

They had a slow and dreamy honeymoon on a boat that made its leisurely way through the Java Sea to Bali. They arrived on the island to encounter total silence and the absence of people, as it was the Balinese New Year. They drove through the island, drinking in the beauty of the delicately changing landscape. They seemed to be drifting through a land of enchantment with its terraced rice fields, gorges, slumbering lanes, and moss-covered temples. Bali was to provide them with what Margaret always regarded as 'the perfect intellectual and emotional working partnership'. The tensions of the Sepik adventure were behind them, she was deeply in love for the first time in her life, and she had a partner whom she respected as an equal. Three years older than her husband, she could no longer regard herself as 'the Punk', although she always insisted that her 'true age' was eleven.

CHAPTER TWO

The Professional

Bali, a small island in Indonesia, was, like Java to the west, at that time part of the Dutch East Indies, which also included Sumatra, the Celebes, and most of Borneo. The Batesons were attracted to it because this jewel in the midst of Muslim Indonesia was famous for its rituals, which pervaded every aspect of daily life. The arts – dance, painting, drama, temple-building – provided the most richly-textured culture they had encountered. Moreover, Bali was civilized, with traditional patterns of behaviour, and over a million people who spoke the same language. There were also congenial Europeans who had been studying the culture and could save the Batesons the arduous task of discovering when particular ceremonies were to take place. The climate was delightful and there were none of the constant discomforts associated with their tedious sojourn on the Sepik. The food was delicious; and unlike her experience on her previous field trips, Margaret did not lose weight. It was the honeymoon period of her life – and it was to last for two delightful years.

They had enthusiastic domestic help. They also had a Balinese 'secretary', I Madé Kaler, who was invaluable to them. Like Banyalo before him, he was initially uneasy about returning to 'inform' on his own people. He had been working as a clerk in Java and had come to look down on the life of the simple mountain peasants, from whom he thought he had escaped. He was now 'hauled back' (how Mead does not specify), but gradually, she asserts, he realized how grateful he was to the Batesons for giving him the opportunity to become reintegrated into his own culture. I Madé Kaler merged into the generally idealized memory of Bali.

Here in a mountain village Mead also had the first and only real home she was ever to have, a house built of pavilions joined by covered walks and furniture made by Balinese craftsmen. After the rigours of New Guinea everything seemed to be accomplished with miraculous ease. At night it was romantically lit by tiny glass lamps.

They were particularly fascinated by the religious observances, a complex blend of animism, Hinduism and Buddhism preserved by historical accident when the rest of the archipelago turned to Islam. They took endless camera shots of the women creating elaborate flower and fruit arrangements for various ceremonies and of the numerous theatrical dances. And on Boas's advice, they concentrated particularly on gesture.

The Batesons had an exciting new research tool – photographic equipment with which to record and describe their observations. Bateson had arrived with seventy-five rolls of 35-millimetre film which soon ran out, and they had to make the decision that it was impossible to proceed without making a major purchase of enough film to last them for over a year. Margaret chose the subjects, Gregory took the pictures, and they developed them together far into the night, eventually washing their faces in the water in which the film had been developed. By the time they left they had accumulated 25,000 photographs. From these they eventually selected the photographs for their joint book, *Balinese Character*, a collection of thematically related stills. The photography was an unprecedentedly ambitious undertaking, although it was not to result in any discoveries of consequence. Nor were they able to come to any vital conclusions about their main project, the cultural aspects of schizophrenia, for which they had been given their basic research funds. The Balinese succeeded in totally defeating them by their ability to withdraw into puzzling self-isolation when bombarded by persistent questions.

It was in Bali that Mead first met her strong-willed agnostic mother-in-law, Beatrice Bateson, accompanied by a friend, Nora Barlow, a granddaughter of Charles Darwin who came to stay with them for six weeks. The two women seemed to get along satisfactorily, particularly as Mrs Bateson threw herself enthusiastically into the life of the island.

At the end of two years it was time to move on. The Batesons had accumulated masses of data about the Balinese, far more than they could ever assimilate. Boas had assured Mead that it would be possible to work in Indonesia without an extensive knowledge of Indian religions. As their ship passed through Torres Strait in March 1938, Mead wrote to him that scholars who approached everything in Bali from the standpoint of a knowledge of Hinduism and Buddhism 'very often miss the essence of it altogether'. This sounds dangerously like a rationalization of the confusion she was experiencing. 'I am still not perfectly clear in my mind about the problem of tackling these complex cultures and the legitimacy of different types of cross-sectioning.' Little wonder that it was with a sense of relief that she headed back to the relative simplicity of New Guinea!

Perhaps, they told themselves, it might be helpful to compare Bali with another culture in order to extract some real significance from it. They decided to return to New Guinea for a brief re-examination of the Iatmul. Mead's relief was enormous. She felt at ease because Bateson was already familiar with the language and the customs of the people. With the outbreak of World War II they were unable to do more than assemble *The Balinese Character*; and Bateson and Mead were never again to work together as a team.

The Batesons were now faced with some major decisions. Margaret understood Bateson's decision to return to his own country, where he felt that he might be of some use in the war effort. After several miscarriages, she found that she was pregnant. It was a joyous discovery, and a great relief for someone who felt compelled always to plan every detail of her life. As for Gregory, he was 'completely pleased and non-ambivalent'. She had chosen the father for her child with the deliberation with which she had selected a partner in the field. In the same rational spirit, the Batesons decided that, given the different cultural conditions, if it were a boy they would settle in England, if a girl in America.

Mary Catherine Bateson was born on 8 December 1939. A young paediatrician, Benjamin Spock (who was chosen because he had been psychoanalysed!), was persuaded to allow the birth to be filmed, and Catherine became the first renowned Spock child. She was addressed as 'Sugar' until it was finally decided that she should be named after Margaret's sister Katherine, who had died in infancy. Before the birth of her baby Margaret had declared that she would assume complete care of the child for the first six months, but within a fortnight she realized that she couldn't be Super Mom, hold down a job at the Museum, nurse the baby, and be up at all hours of the night. Determined to be as natural with her child as the native women she had observed, at first she industriously set about breast-feeding her baby although she never found the experience particularly fulfilling. She also had the loving ministrations of her devoted friend, Marie Eichelberger, whose apartment they shared, but there was general relief when an experienced English nanny was hired to take over the caretaking of the infant. From her Cathy received 'slightly astringent affection'.

Bateson found that there seemed nothing of any urgency that required him to be in wartime England, away from his family. On hearing the good news, Mead wrote ecstatically to her husband, 'Oh darling, it will be heaven to have you back again, to bring up the baby together.' On his return to New York he and Margaret spent a weekend looking after Catherine; 'very much like playing house with a doll', he recalled – although dolls don't suffer from inconvenient ailments like colic. They then began a long series of experiments in communal living, at first with Lawrence and Mary Frank and their five children in a house in Greenwich Village, of which they occupied two floors. The summers were spent in the Franks' large house near Holderness, New Hampshire, where they were joined by Bateson's teenage British god-daughters, the Guillebauds, for the duration of the war. Mead sent their economist father in Cambridge regular reports on the girls' daily routine and progress. At first she found them as strange as the Mundugumor, until she devised ingenious games as a means of breaking down their reserve. 'They had no idea of the kind of initiative that America children do,' she complained. She had a normative view of American behaviour against which others were implicitly judged. To distract the children from the war, they banned the radio from the house and only occasionally glanced at a newspaper.

In 1942 her first mentor, Franz Boas, dropped dead at a luncheon where he was the guest speaker. All his works had been removed from the library at the University of Kiev (where he had received his doctorate in 1881) because the Nazis found particularly distasteful his opposition to the theory of 'Aryan' racial superiority, a theory which formed the basis of the National Socialist philosophy.

After the bombing of Pearl Harbor at the beginning of 1942, the Museum gave Mead full-time wartime leave of absence to organize the National Research Council's Committee on Food Habits. This was one of the vague fact-finding agencies assigned to 'experts'. She and four other anthropologists worked with the Committee for National Morale. In general these were investigations into 'national character', based largely on the work of Geoffrey Gorer's study of the Japanese through interviews with missionaries and a study of the country's literature. When Gorer moved to the British Embassy wartime staff he nominated Ruth Benedict to replace him, and she remained in Washington for the duration of the war. It was not until a visit to Europe in 1948 that she was reassured to find that the actual Poles, Czechs, Dutch and Belgians were much as she had described them.

Bateson, too, was working in Washington, in the Office of Strategic Services; but in February 1944 he was sent to the Far East for the duration, an altogether miserable period for him. He was so depressed that months would pass without Mead ever receiving a letter from him.

In 1943 Mead made a trip (or 'mission') to England on her own. The purpose was somewhat vague: to understand the problems the GIs were experiencing in courting English girls. She seemed more bemused by the English than by any exotic tribe in the heart of New Guinea. Queues were a curious social custom to her. She was puzzled by the English passion for gardening; and when she was taken to visit the exquisite Sussex garden of anthropologist Geoffrey Gorer (who was later to become a close friend), she refused to inspect it. Nevertheless, every time Gorer and his guests raised their heads they caught Mead watching them from different windows in the house. Later, when teased about this, she replied, 'I just wanted to see how English people talked to each other about gardening.'

Her notebook always at the ready, Mead announced to the Barlow family, whom she was visiting, that she was going to observe Nora Barlow's three-year-old granddaughter and a little friend playing together. The children froze under her steely gaze peering at them through her rimless spectacles. Mead returned to the adults with the announcement, 'English children don't talk.' But for someone who enjoyed being observed as much as observing, she complained to her husband, 'I am getting a little tired of being an exhibit in Anglo-American relations every minute of the day.' It was a rather self-absorbed remark, considering that the British were enduring the Blitz at the time.

During the war Mead published *And Keep Your Powder Dry* (1942), most of which she wrote while commuting between Washington and New York. In her Preface she described it as 'a social scientist's contribution to winning the war and establishing a just and lasting peace'. Absorbed as she had been in her own 'peoples', she was never to indicate much interest in political questions, and during the thirties she had not been caught up with Communism or with the Spanish Civil War. But now, after seventeen years' experience of other cultures, she felt qualified to re-examine her own with fresh eyes. Published in England as *The American Character*, it was also an attempt to explain the Americans to the British. It turned out to be the first of many books which were to make her into a universal guru. Its platitudinous observations and tone of total confidence appealed to what Ruth Benedict described as 'Macy shoppers'. She had gained the confidence to speak with authority on every subject under the sun. As Mead once remarked, 'The whole world is my field. It's all anthropology.' Here she was following the dictum of her mentor, Ruth Benedict, that 'culture is personality writ large'. Mead typified the new breed of anthropologist in her belief that the various 'races' of mankind are specializations without measurable differences.

On Margaret's return to England, Cathy, who had felt abandoned, snubbed her mother. No one had thought to mention to her that Mead's return had been postponed from summer until late fall. Mead absorbed the lesson, and in future informed her daughter about her plans as precisely as possible.

In childhood Catherine Bateson grew accustomed to

seeing her mother only irregularly, and a three-day period they shared together was something of an event. At the time Mead justified this by a public statement: 'I think I lose something by that arrangement, but I'm pretty sure she doesn't.' Mead was always absolutely sure that whatever she did was the right thing – from the discarding of husbands to the advantages of an extended family where there were always other people around to attend to the irritating practical details. She never tired of castigating the 'nuclear family', although her own life style could not have been maintained without a network whose reliability she could count on. She always had the ability to attract to her people willing to be, as one intimate friend described it, 'slaves'. She would suggest to friends that they be psychoanalysed, but she never admitted to feeling it necessary for herself; although, according to Mary Catherine Bateson, she was advised to go to an analyst when it was clear that her own marriage was deteriorating. But this need for help was not acknowledged, and introspection was never a temptation for her.

The furnishings of the Bateson quarters in the house on Perry Street were plain, adorned with only a few reproductions on the walls. Mead had collected few artefacts for herself on her field trips. In these years her appearance became more and more schoolmarmish – something the American public seemed to like. What mattered most to her was energy, and the house was bursting with noise – people constantly coming and going, and talk over the table long after dinner was finished. Psychologist Marie Jahoda remembers her inveterate talk as spontaneous and original, 'things you had never thought of before'. While she dominated the conversation, 'she involved herself with absolutely everything in the universe. She just confronted the world as a whole. In many ways it was superficial, but the flashes came out. It's good to have a human being who tries to take in the whole.' Dr Carol Kaye, a psychoanalyst (who had been Mead's secretary from 1947 to 1950), recalls that she always looked forward to seeing her because she added so much zest to life. 'One could talk to her at such complex levels. She always had something rich and generous to say.'

It was a reasonably happy period, punctuated by Mead's frequent bouts of irritation when small items of life did not respond adequately to her bidding. She observed her child's development with close attention, and, like her mother, kept intensive notes. An easel was placed beside Cathy's bed so that she could paint her dreams on awakening. Mead taught her daughter to watch the domestic habits of other families they visited. All this attention was particularly necessary during the war when Bateson was away, and Mead felt very lonely when he didn't write during his periods of despondency. A displaced wife during wartime was too unstructured a role for her liking.

Mead and Bateson were able to work together in isolation in the field, but intolerable pressures were put on the partnership once they tried to establish a relatively normal family life after the war. Mead was thoroughly at home in New York. She had her secure job at the Museum of Natural History, a wide network of supportive friends, and the status of a national celebrity. Bateson was just as hungry for recognition as his wife, but there was no way he could compete with her. 'It was almost a principle of pure energy,' he recalled ruefully. 'I couldn't keep up and she couldn't stop.'

Mead always insisted on courtesy, ritual, and appearance, but in many ways she was totally insensitive to the feelings of others – particularly of her own husband. In 1946, when Bateson was lecturing at the New School of Social Research, she started to attend his classes, settling in the middle of the hall and never hesitating to interrupt when she disagreed with him. 'No, Gregory, that wasn't the way it was at all.' Eventually she took over the class and he retreated, baffled and angry.

Despite the illusions of their early relationship, their thinking diverged in totally different directions. Gregory's habit of drawing far-fetched analogies irritated Margaret, who did not disguise the fact that she thought he suffered from muddle-headed laziness. Games such as charades were part of the summer routine in New England among the social scientists, but there was little fun in the marriage. A film could not simply be enjoyed, but had to be scrupulously analysed from a professional perspective. The immense difference in their heights seemed paradigmatic of the pair. A familiar image of the couple was of Mead striding ahead of her husband, talking a mile a minute, while a silent Bateson lagged behind.

Women found him immensely attractive. 'He was irresistible,' Marie Jahoda recalled. By now it was clear that he was having affairs. Mead always maintained that jealousy was culturally induced; but she was heard to remark plaintively that she didn't know what Gregory saw in 'those girls'. In order to keep Cathy from knowing of the tensions in the marriage, Mead did not even confide in loyal Aunt Marie Eichelberger. Obsessional about extracting confidences from others, she seemed to think that she would lose some of her authority if she revealed even a chink of vulnerability. However, from the time she was two Cathy was aware that something was wrong, and on one occasion found her mother at the window choking back the tears.

Eventually Bateson moved out to Staten Island, but he found that wasn't sufficiently distant from Margaret's network. Later he went to the west coast to work on a study of human communication, which in turn led to further research into animal behaviour, particularly his famous study of dolphins. After three years of separation he informed Mead bluntly by telephone that he wanted a divorce in order to remarry. This was the first time any of her husbands had left her, one of the few times Mead had not been able to order life as she wished; and she never fully recovered from the hurt and bewilderment. One of her ways of coping with it was the defence of denial. She declared that divorce was no more a failure than death and that marriage, like parenthood, was a vocation. In 1949 in *Male and Female* she took the opportunity to write, 'The expectation of permanency is still great enough to brand every impermanence as a failure, if not a sin, and also because to all the other insecurities of American life, insecurity about marriage is added.' In old age she angered a number of people when she announced that divorce was a moral act.

There is no doubt that Mead was very much in love with Bateson and anxious to keep an openness in their relationship. She made a determined effort to ensure that the divorce would cause as little disruption as possible in Cathy's life. Mead flew out to the west coast where the child was staying with her father so that they could jointly break the news to her. This they did during a walk in the park where they were having a picnic. The little ten-year-old lay down on the ground and cried inconsolably.

A new pattern of life had to be created. Mead and her daughter moved into a house in Waverly Place in the Village. This was the home of fellow-anthropologist Rhoda Metraux, who was to share Mead's life and much of her work in subsequent years. Cathy was sent to the fashionable Brearley School. She continued to spend weekends with the invaluable Aunt Marie, who even kept needles threaded for Margaret, who refused to learn any practical task that bored her.

Mary Catherine Bateson has recorded that her life with her parents was punctuated with departures; and her childhood bitterness at having felt abandoned breaks through her scrupulous attempt to weigh motive and reaction equably. On her visits to her father she developed a mature relationship in which he would talk to her as an adult about natural history, a subject about which her mother was abysmally ignorant. Their camping trips were just part of the general relaxed manner of Bateson's whole life, of which Mead disapproved. Bateson was interested in finding stray animals, Mead in collecting people, including fifty relatives, the necessary adjunct of her extended family, who in turn were studied like any tribe.

In New York an orderly pattern of life was strenuously cultivated. Birthday parties had to be planned months in advance. In the complicated schedule of their lives elaborate planning was absolutely necessary, such as the procedure when Cathy was put on a plane to be met by her father when she visited him in California. Mead had begun a perpetual round of lecturing and conferences. The museum allowed her an extraordinary amount of flexibility, which she used to her advantage by avoiding administrative work while remaining for years at the level of associate curator. Cathy accompanied her on a three-month tour to Australia in 1951. In New Zealand she encountered Reo Fortune whom, she told her daughter, she hadn't considered suitable as a father. Cathy grew up as a well-behaved child, knowing full well the penalty of naughtiness or defiance. 'I can't come home to this kind of thing,' Mead complained after one incident of childish mischief. The worst thing she could be was 'boring'. Occasionally she startled her mother when she was very little with remarks such as 'I want to eat Mummy', and sometimes her aggressive play intimidated other children.

When Cathy was about eight years old her mother decided upon an ingenious scheme for teaching her how to use language. With Mead sitting at the typewriter, Cathy would dictate, Mead supplying the punctuation from the rhythms of her voice. She also taught her daughter how to divide thought into paragraphs, and Cathy Bateson has recalled the delight of the instruction: 'Parenthesis!'

Mead's Christianity never faltered. It provided a touchstone in her life of perpetual motion. Her religion seemed a necessary part of the interweaving strands of her life. 'Networking' was not simply an aim in itself. Many have spoken of her great depth of empathy: and for some her understanding of others reached the level of genius. Friendship, particularly with Ruth Benedict, was invested with an air of sanctity. And the religion they both shared was anthropology, which they disseminated with proselytizing zeal.

Everything, as they saw it, was anthropology. 'I've at last discovered,' Mead told the anthropologist R. L. B. Birdwhistell, 'that I have been studying all my life, not cultural anthropology, nor yet culture and personality, but human evolution. It all fits together.' Perhaps her great popular appeal lay in her vernacular stress on actual people and recognizable relationships. 'For me,' she told Radcliffe-Brown, 'the most important thing in science is to study realities (real objects and real events) and to talk about them in terms of abstractions but not to treat abstractions as though they were realities . . . Our realities are individuals and their actions and the relations between individuals . . .'

Mead had no compunction about addressing herself to everything under the sun, laying herself open to the charge of pretentiousness. She became even more visible as a TV personality and as a columnist for *Redbook* magazine. No audience seemed big enough for her. Many of her colleagues were unimpressed. They felt that such publicity was self-promoting and tended to trivialize her discipline. One of them describes her as proffering ideas like mannequins in a fashion book, pausing when she recognized that she had touched a responsive chord. She was perhaps most effective at the small conference where she could encourage each participant to make his particular contribution, and she herself was especially effective in cutting through the data to isolate and identify specific problems. She was impressive in her openness to thinking in many different frames of reference.

In 1948 Ruth Benedict died. Mead wept frantically at the funeral for the person she had probably loved the most in life. People recognized the depth of her grief and letters of sympathy poured in. She confided in one friend that 'Ruth

65

Benedict's death has disorganized my life at practically every level.' She later declared airily that 'When people die, I have no sense that I have lost them.' Nevertheless, her biography of Benedict (1974) was in a sense an attempt to keep Benedict alive for ever. She was very careful, however, that no one could read it as a personal memoir. Mead had always been fiercely defensive of Benedict's professionalism and of her importance as one of the first women to attain major stature as a social scientist. She was fiercely defensive of Benedict's differentiation of cultures, which Radcliffe-Brown had described as the 'rags and tatters' approach of historical diffusionism. Mead set out to justify the way she had used Nietzsche's terms 'Apollonian' and 'Dionysian' in *Patterns of Culture* and had applied 'paranoid' and 'megalomaniac' in her characterization of the Dobuan and Kwakiutl cultures. Mead's argument that these terms had a specific theoretical orientation for Benedict was an implausible justification for convenient demarcations; and Mead was on much stronger ground in her account of the hostility Benedict had to struggle against from the anthropological establishment in obtaining research funds and in her advancement within the hierarchy at Columbia.

In 1949 one of her Columbia graduate students, Harold Gerard, impressed her with a study he had done of the famous textile strike in Lowell, Mass. by the IWW in 1912. She invited him to spend a day with her in the museum to observe how she functioned. He was 'absolutely awed' by her energy and her verbal felicity. She suggested that he go off and do field work. His new wife strenuously objected. What could Mead do for him then? Gerard said that he wanted to go to the University of Michigan to study with the psychologist Ronald Lippett. She picked up the telephone and it was arranged. There are innumerable stories of her giving help of this kind.

While many people felt that they were friends of Margaret Mead, all of them had to be useful, most of them as informants in one capacity or another. Her rationale for not returning to places she had studied before was that they had nothing new to teach her. However, she was persuaded in 1953 to revisit Manus, where she learned that a politician named Paliau was instigating far-reaching changes in the island which Mead had tended to regard as frozen in time. A new era in her life was initiated with her return to this field. 'It is time to go back,' this most urban of women told people. 'We've run out of ideas.'

## CHAPTER THREE

## Grandmother to the World

'I have come back,' Mead told the people of Peré, 'because of the great speed with which you have changed, and in order to find out more about how people change so that this knowledge can be used all over the world.' She also realized that the theoretical base of anthropology had undergone significant modifications and that it was necessary to return to the 'laboratories in the jungle'.

The expedition involved the complicated planning that Margaret always loved. The most important priority was to find a companion who was both congenial and adequately qualified to cope with a wide variety of challenges. A nation-wide search resulted in the selection of twenty-five-year-old Theodore Schwartz and his new wife (Mead warned them that life in the field put a strain on marriage). After months of intensive preparation, the trio arrived on Manus island in June 1953.

The people Mead had described in *Growing Up in New Guinea* had been changed irrevocably by the American occupation of the Admiralty Islands. Mead set herself to answer certain questions: how had these people managed to come so swiftly into the twentieth century and how were they coping with it?

In the years since her original visit she had matured and gained great self-confidence. She had been open to all sorts of new ideas which could be useful in understanding a culture: psychoanalysis, clinical psychology, semiotics, cybernetics. With such a background she could not possibly take as simplistic an approach as she had done in the past.

Mead found herself in a situation much like meeting cousins one hadn't seen for twenty-five years. In the months she spent there she came to the conclusion, which she elaborated in *New Lives for Old* (1956), that it is easier to adapt to rapid change than to slow and partial transition. From Peré she wrote to a friend, 'I feel closer to a people who believe that they can remake their culture if only they have the will to do so.' This, in the fortunate case of the Manus, was due to their dynamic leader, Paliau, who was determined to bring all the peoples of Manus into a democratic society capable of dealing with modern life. Although an old man told her on her departure, 'Now, like an old turtle, you are going out to the sea to die and we will never see you again,' Mead was to return many times to Manus, for here she found reinforcement for her belief that men can learn to change, 'quickly, happily, without violence, without madness, without coercion, and of their own free will'. It was a message of hope and optimism for America.

It was an exciting period of re-evaluation for Mead. The Manus had discarded their shell money, native dress, arranged marriages, and ancient ceremonies. The children no longer smoked or chewed betel nut. The villages were now resettled on land, with the houses designed on European models. Each village had a democratically elected assembly. Mead was aware that this transformation could not have been possible if the Americans had not left behind plywood and other materials. Her emotions were deeply stirred, hope mingled with an unmistakable nostalgia for the past which she tried to control. 'The whole thing is fascinating, a little heartbreaking, but also something that makes one proud of the human race. I think I can give an account of it all that will make sense to Americans, give them some new sense of the new things that are stirring in the minds of backward peoples everywhere.'

There was cleanliness but a certain individual style was lost for ever. All was for the good, she told herself. She was disturbed by the loss of the old cultural complexity but moved by what seemed a gentle spiritual transformation. Things had to be black or white. 'I am no longer distressed by the children's screams in the night. This is learned behaviour, an aggressive assertion of their dislike of waking up or of a desire to sleep with a different parent, etc.' When she encountered depression or young men intending suicide, she realized that she must impress upon them that they represented the hope of the future. All this meant a significant difference to the anthropologist, who must participate rather than simply observe. Such a role undoubtedly suited Mead, who was never averse to telling people how to run their lives.

In 1965 she returned to Peré alone – the first time she had been completely alone on a field trip since Samoa. She was surrounded by people whose past she knew better than they themselves, and she was living in relative comfort. Nevertheless, she reflected about field work, the extraordinary vocation it was, and the incredible demands it made on a young field worker. All in all, it was 'a rather appalling thing to undertake'. It was not surprising that her thoughts turned in this direction because she had recently been in Australia, where anthropologist Derek Freeman was beginning to question seriously the findings made by a twenty-six-year-old so very, very long ago.

Ted and Lenora Schwartz found Mead an exacting person to work with. She was to change their lives irrevocably, but it was a hard course. Schwartz grew accustomed to receiving notes from her about the 'scalding bad temper' into which he had plunged her because of his inefficiency. She sometimes conveyed the impression that she was the only person in the world who knew how to get things done. The tension always present in her office in the museum accompanied her wherever she went. The demand for perfection, the rapid changes of mood, the towering temper, bound some people closely to her in their desire to please her; others were alienated permanently. To those whom she wished to help she gave generously, securing research grants or publishers (particularly for her former husbands) and listening intently to their troubles. But she could be harsh to those who opposed her, in some cases even threatening to destroy their careers. She enjoyed heckling audiences but could easily be discomfited, even reduced to tears, by being heckled herself or, on occasion, booed.

In 1956 she took Cathy on a trip to Israel. Here Mead worked as a consultant on the assimilation of immigrants with different cultural backgrounds. From this experience, combined with that of the Manus, she produced a book, *Culture and Commitment*, on the theme of the way the young learn from each other in a society which does not provide older models. Cathy meanwhile travelled around with young people visiting kibbutzim. She fell in love with the country and Mead agreed to let her stay, learn Hebrew, and matriculate from a Hebrew high school. Actually she had little choice, because it was clear that Cathy had a will as strong as her own. It must have been difficult for Mead to give Cathy her freedom – for this was in effect what she was doing – and they never lived together again. Motherhood had provided her with the authority to don the role of world spokesperson on parenting and child development. In *Blackberry Winter* Mead speaks of her early anxiety that she might be an over-protective mother, and now she heeded her own warning.

Cathy felt an immense sense of relief in being able to create a life for herself, for she realized that she had to be more than an adjunct to a famous mother. She appreciated the pride and immense affection her mother felt for her pretty daughter, but she had to get away. After Mead's death she was clearly torn between passionate loyalty and a sense of shock that her mother pursued bisexual relationships. She realized clearly how important it was to Mead, the observer, how she was *perceived*. Mead felt that even though she was the most visible of public presences, there were aspects of her private life into which no one had any right to penetrate. During these years she had a recurrent fantasy of how one might disappear without trace. Nevertheless, she took a certain mischievous delight in the knowledge that people gossiped about her sex life, and it didn't bother her at all if it was rumoured to be somewhat lurid. After all, it was part of the myth. Better to be talked about than to be ignored.

Did she ever feel a victim of her own driving energy for

success? During the years of what she described as her 'post-menopausal zest', Mead became the centre of attention at interdisciplinary conferences, TV interviews, and lecture engagements (sixty or so a year). Wherever she went she took with her a small silk pillow which allowed her to drop asleep on planes or in hotel rooms. One colleague remarked that when one entered a restaurant, Mead's voice could be heard above all the rest, her face growing ruddier with the passing years.

In addition to her work at the American Museum of Natural History she lectured at Columbia, where she never became more than an adjunct professor. She served on innumerable committees, received twenty-seven honorary degrees, and was finally made a full curator at the museum. By the time she was offered tenure at Columbia she was too famous to need it. Students remembered her lectures as travelogues, and some faculty members did not hide their disapproval of her tendency to popularize her material. She airily overlooked the reactions of her peers. What she wanted was universal acclaim.

However, she was at her best in small groups where she would introduce a new idea which would inspire people from diverse backgrounds and interests to dissect and elaborate. This sort of setting was provided for her at the Menninger Foundation in Topeka, Kansas, which from 1959 she visited regularly as a 'consultant'. Her early hostility to psychoanalysis had long since abated. If ideas were stimulating and useful, they were grist for her mill.

She declared that one three-month period she spent at the Menninger was 'exceedingly useful' and that it provided her with a whole set of new insights into what Freud 'really meant' in *Totem and Taboo*.

She counted a large number of psychoanalysts among her admirers. Erik Erikson was particularly close to her, discussing with her ideas he was developing in *Identity and the Life Cycle*. Mead wrote to him after reading the section on trust: 'I suspect that it is easier to purposively cultivate trustworthiness than it is to purposively cultivate trust. Think it over.' He sent her the manuscript of *Young Man Luther* for her detailed comments. When it was published in 1958 she helped publicize it with a description of it as 'a unique integration of psychoanalysis, history, and the problem of the Great Man focused upon a central question of our time, the question of individual identity'.

She did not have the same warmth of feeling for Bruno Bettelheim. When he published *Symbolic Wounds* in 1954 she was furious that the material in a chapter on *couvade*, a symbolic ceremony in which males invest themselves with the creative, life-giving power of the female, had been gleaned from *Male and Female* (1949) without any acknowledgement.

While the 1953 field trip to Manus was the last one in which Mead did the major share of the work, air travel enabled her to make frequent relatively short forays in the next twenty years, although none of them long enough for any coordinated investigation. As she had always done in the past, she continued to wear cotton dresses that had to be laundered and ironed daily. While most of her trips were to Manus, she also joined Rhoda Metraux in Montserrat and New Guinea. In 1971 on a return flight from New Guinea she stopped for five days in Samoa, where she officially opened a power plant. On a trip to Bali in 1977 she refused to admit that anything had changed. Possibly she was projecting her own fear of death, her refusal to accept that she herself was different.

As she grew older religion played an even more important part in her life, and she lived the vows she had made in that confirmation service when she was eleven. Ritual in everyday life was always important to her; and it was particularly important in binding people together in what she called 'a cosmic sense'. In the numerous homes she stayed in during her travels her hosts were often amazed on a Sunday morning when she would slip out of the house to attend an Episcopalian service. In 1961 she was very concerned that her three divorces might prevent her from representing the Episcopalian Church of the United States on the Committee for Assembly of the World Council of Churches. She was delighted when the issue did not arise. This involvement was particularly important to her at a time when the ecumenical movement was posing questions about collective Christian worship. She enthusiastically attended seven annual conferences, and recorded her enthusiasm for these ventures in her last book, *World Enough: Rethinking the Future.*

Celebrations, pageants, anniversaries enabled Mead to keep in touch with her extended family – all her own relatives, the relatives of her divorced husbands, the Ash Can Cats, the friends she inevitably collected at congresses. Every year her Christmas card list grew longer and longer. American audiences loved her because she encouraged fellowship, caring, and friendship – all the things Americans did best. She also reassured them that failure was only the inability to think positively. These values she herself needed badly when her sister Priscilla committed suicide in 1959. That year she wrote to Erik Erikson: 'Life is good but terribly

terribly thick, and full of prickly problems – other peoples'.'
In a sense she was the female counterpart of Norman
Vincent Peale. And in her flowing cape and with the
forked cherrywood stick that she now carried with her everywhere, she spoke and looked like a prophet, a role she found
particularly satisfying. Americans liked her for being fat and
plain. People frequently told her that she reminded them of
their mothers.

While her help to others was wide and eclectic, she also
demanded much; yet she prevented anyone from coming
too close to her, thus allowing a mystique to become attached to her person. In a sense her appeal lay in a certain
philistine quality which she carefully cultivated. She seemed
to take perverse pleasure in mispronouncing foreign words.
While she had been an ardent theatre-goer as a student at
Barnard, in mid-life she could not sit still long enough to
watch a play. She read *The New York Times* from cover to
cover every day, but only to extract information which
would be useful in her work. Science fiction was about the
only form of relaxation she would allow herself. 'Luckily,'
she opined, 'I do not distinguish between work and pleasure,
and I seldom have to do anything I don't want to do.'

By 1970, when it was very clear that a feminist revolution
was under way, Mead poured scorn on the middle-aged
women who complained that they had been victimized by a
male-dominated society because, so far as she could see, they
had passively allowed themselves to be the objects of dis-
crimination.

She would not allow herself to join in the chorus of vituper-
ation against Freud. While agreeing that he was naïve about
women, she pointed out that the social definitions of male

and female roles throughout history have reflected practical conditions. She argued that those who had studied children in other societies (for example Mead herself) were indebted to him because they were aware of the rhythms of human development. It could be highly dangerous to introduce artificial intervention into natural processes, to interfere with traditionally established patterns. There was a certain inconsistency here. Mead had praised the people of Manus for their swift adaptation to modern life.

Betty Friedan, in *The Feminine Mystique*, attacked Mead, particularly for her sexual stereotyping in *Male and Female*. Friedan shrewdly perceived that Mead divided women into two categories – on the one hand, childbearing, supportive wives, and on the other, rare individualists like herself. And that is just the way Margaret Mead wanted it to be. If all women had the same freedom as herself, she wouldn't have stood out in the crowd. Mead never hesitated to take advantage of being a woman. She found it far more convenient not to be able to drive a car; it was more productive for her in field work to concentrate on women and children. Similarly, she took no part in a whole range of activities such as sport. She concentrated only on those things in which she felt confident that she could excel.

If women had certain strengths, they had weaknesses as well. She turned down the presidency of a large university on the grounds that women make poor administrators. She noted that women seemed sadder and more dissatisfied than men, but she took it for granted that this was simply the way things were. Nevertheless, she always preferred lecturing to women and having women work for her. There seems little doubt that there was a strong bisexual element in her preferences, although she also enjoyed the company of homosexual men. For some years, for instance, there was a persistent rumour that she would marry her frequent companion, Geoffrey Gorer.

Although Mead never held any pretensions about being a scholar (as distinct from being sure she was right about everything), she was offended that the universality of her fame did not always endear her to her peers. She did not increase her popularity among them by her announcement that 'our colleges were 400 years out of date', or by favouring a coed draft, although she added the caveat that she would not give guns to women because 'they are too fierce'.

It was a matter of some grievance to her that she was not elected to membership in the National Academy of Sciences, although her name had been proposed a number of times. She was under suspicion for the column in *Redbook* and for her willingness to remain what she considered open-minded about parapsychology and unidentified flying objects. Sensitive to criticism, she declared, 'The entire scientific world is a hierarchy of snobbery . . . Each science looks down on the newer ones, the newer ones being far more difficult and complicated than the old ones.'

In old age she could not complain of not receiving the attention due to her. On her seventy-fifth birthday, 16 December 1976, she opened the *New York Times* to encounter a full-page advertisement: 'HAPPY BIRTHDAY MARGARET MEAD.' She thought of the perfect remark to reporters to quote: 'I expect to die, but I don't plan to retire.'

Despite the public acclaim, there were many who were

disenchanted with her, especially those who considered her views as glib and naïve. This was confirmed by *A Rap on Race* with James Baldwin in 1970. To Baldwin's heartfelt assertion that he would never feel at home anywhere on this earth, she snapped, 'Fiddlesticks!' Many people became convinced that she seemed totally oblivious to the plight of the blacks. Her attitude seemed to suggest that they didn't possess a positive enough attitude. Nevertheless she genuinely believed that 'Too much emphasis on the spurious nature of racial classification by antisegregationists could backfire into emasculating the very necessary attempts to build up political responsibility, internal cohesion, and activism in Negro groups.' It took courage in 1968 in a volume, *Science and the Concept of Race*, to declare that too much emphasis on race in political terms might lead to the absurdity of an editorial in the *Daily News* which accused Adam Clayton Powell of merely 'passing' as a black because he had three white grandparents.

She maintained a good relationship with Cathy, possibly because they saw each other only intermittently. And yet, in recalling her mother's life of perpetual movement, Cathy reflected with quiet sadness that 'She would not simply stay to be loved.' At Radcliffe, Cathy met an Armenian engineering student, Barkev Kassarjian, whom she married just after graduation. She, too, married into a different culture, but one that she had been prepared for by her sojourn in the Middle East. At the wedding Gregory stood in the receiving line in a tailcoat. Margaret was naturally the centre of attention, in a wheelchair to which she had been confined after a fall.

Cathy and Barkev spent much of the next twenty years in

the Philippines and Iran. Sometimes Mead would sign a letter to her with a curt, professional 'MM', not noticing what she had done. In 1974 she and Geoffrey Gorer visited Cathy and her husband in Teheran, using the occasion to exchange ideas with local anthropologists. Cathy found that the advantage of living in these places was that there was so much that was unfamiliar to Mead that, for lack of understanding of the culture, she could not try to arrange their lives for them. Cathy had learned early that the only way she might achieve real independence was by being as far away from her mother as possible.

She was also aware that even a daughter would satisfy only a small portion of Mead's need for relationships. When they did meet, there was an orgy of talk. Cathy realized that it was not necessary to read all her mother's books, although Mead assiduously read everything that Cathy wrote. Interestingly, Cathy also made an exploratory journey back into the Episcopalian Church. All these aspects of her relationship with her mother she discusses frankly in *With a Daughter's Eye*, as well as the stifling effect Mead had on her husbands. In this book, written after her mother's death, she reveals that she felt somewhat betrayed because Mead had deceived her about her current sexual relationships, and also saddened because her mother had not felt close enough to her to confide in her.

This sense of secrecy was preserved because Mead was determined that no breath of scandal should touch her now that her three marriages were behind her. Her autobiography, *Blackberry Winter*, appeared in 1972 with the subtitle *My Earlier Years*, but she never intended to write a sequel. The book ends with a long account of being a mother and a grandmother – and this section, too, might have been contrived as part of the mosaic of her public image, for Mead never had the public long out of mind.

In 1966 Mead and Rhoda Metraux moved from the Village to an apartment in the Beresford on Central Park West within easy walking distance of the museum. While the apartment was in Metraux's name, a friend recalls that it was very much a teacher-disciple relationship. 'Rhoda, get the tea,' Mead would order her. There were stormy sessions, and for a time Mead moved out.

In 1955 Mead sent a letter addressed 'to those I love'. It was a leave-taking in case she should die suddenly, and an apologia for the compartmentalization of her life:

I prefer a life in which each important feeling and thought can be shared with someone whom one loves, friend or spouse – several friends, teachers and pupils. It has not been my choice of concealment that anyone of you has been left in ignorance of some part of my life which would seem, I know, of great importance. Nor has it been from lack of trust – in any person – on my part, but only from the exigencies of the mid-twentieth century which each one of us – at least those of us who are my age – seems fated for a life which is no longer sharable.

In 1969 Cathy's daughter, Vanni, was born. Mead was now old enough to have been a great-grandmother. It was startling to discover herself biologically related to a new human being. This introduced an entirely new element into her observational bias. Again, as she had been aware of her tendency to be an over-protective mother, she had to school herself not to be an interfering grandmother. To Bateson she reported: 'The baby flourishes, and is gaining very fast, and is plump and very very alert and sensitive, responsive to pattern. Definitely a descendant.'

Mead was beginning to wind down. In 1978 her major plan was a trip to New Guinea before the end of the year. All her life there had been complicated plans for the future, but now they were assuming an air of fantasy. She had gained so much weight in recent years that she had difficulty fastening the seat belt on aeroplanes: suddenly it became apparent that she was losing weight at an alarming rate. On 12 April (as always her notes were dated) in a memorandum to herself, after a medical consultation, she wrote: 'Mass on the body of the pancreas most likely represents a malignancy.' Her brother Richard had already died of the same ailment. The dread word 'cancer' was never used, and she even tried to persuade herself and a number of her friends that she was suffering from anorexia nervosa. Bateson was already diagnosed for cancer the same year and for a long time she persuaded herself that he was far more ill than she, although he had a remarkable remission before his death in 1980. She was Margaret Mead and nothing was going to defeat her. However, she did seek help in a rather unexpected quarter. This she found in a faith healer, a Chilean woman who called herself the Reverend Carmen di Barazza. Mead's confidence in this large, enveloping woman was total, touching, and disturbing.

In early August, Mead actually organized a conference on the future at Chautauqua. It was the first and only time she, Gregory, and Cathy had been together as colleagues, and the occasion clearly had great symbolic value for Mead. Photographs show a different woman – sombre and withdrawn. Cathy cared for her as tenderly as a child. Mead made it clear to her daughter that she did not want her to return if she was summoned urgently from Iran with the news that her mother's condition was deteriorating.

Her final illness was not her greatest hour. She did not go easily into the great unknown. During the last years her outspokenness had too often become arrogance and surliness. While she was brave about pain, she was angry that she could no longer control her life. Her sense of omnipotence was such that only at the end did she admit that she had cancer. She exploded when she discovered that Cathy and Vanni had arrived, because she did not want her granddaughter to see her in such a weakened state in hospital.

Cathy was dismayed to find that she seemed to be surrounded by possessive vultures. 'Around my mother's hospital bed, conflicts flared up between people who had been important in different parts of her life but had no friendship for each other, insisting competitively on a right to a portion of her time and attention, overwhelming any efforts to limit the flow of visitors.' On the morning of 15 November 1978, she died. Always afraid of travelling unaccompanied, her final journey was one she had to make as a solitary soul. Her ashes were buried in the graveyard of the Pennsylvania church where she had been married to Luther and where she had been baptized at the age of eleven. Perhaps she had come home at last.

CHAPTER FOUR

Still Famous

At Mead's memorial service Bateson remarked that it would be difficult to assess specifically what her contributions to social science had been, but they were real nonetheless. Even her most ardent admirers speak glowingly but vaguely about how Mead's place can be assessed.

Perhaps her greatest impact was in the application of her anthropological insight to universal social problems. Her categorical espousal of the primacy of social environment, totally excluding biological variables, became a basic dogma of American cultural anthropology. It is this issue to which Freeman has primarily addressed himself. Nevertheless, *Sex and Temperament*, her advocates claimed, undercut current theories that men are the natural aggressors while women are passive. The way in which the Manus changed from easy-going children into grasping adults made people take a second look at progressive education. Whatever the tenability of her various positions, her work in the field, her books about culture and personality, and her lectures made a very large audience *aware* of these questions.

Margaret Mead came on the scene at a decisive moment in the development of anthropology. Anthropologists were beginning to be driven by a sense of urgency to 'get it all down before it's gone'. Americans in particular had reason to feel anxious as they witnessed the disappearance of the buffalo and rituals such as the potlatch, the North American Indian ceremony of surpassing one's friends in excessive hospitality. A great deal about the Indian had been recorded in the first part of the century, and some anthropologists felt that they had come to the end of the road in recording the history of primitive America. If there was any new work to be done, they had to turn to Africa or Australia or the South Pacific.

'Diffusion' was the buzz word Mead heard in her classes at Columbia. Diffusion, or the tracing of cultural traits around the world, had been initiated by the study of folklore and mythology. A whole new field of investigation gradually began to open up – culture change, or 'acculturation', as it came to be called. Observation began to be stressed more than ever as the prerequisite of field technique. What tools were used in houses? Who was allowed to attend what ceremonies? How were the members of a household related and what was the status of the various individuals?

This latter question focused more attention on the individual within his culture. In what way did he conform to the norms of his society? To what extent was the individual moulded by that culture? What was a deviant?

When Freud's *Totem and Taboo* was published in 1918 it was read by most anthropologists with shocked disbelief. The idea of equating the primitive with the child and the neurotic had been a prejudice that anthropologists had been strenuously trying to eliminate. Now their efforts had to be geared even more to undermining Freud's position. However, there were some people with more open minds, some who believed that anthropology and psychoanalysis could learn from each other. One of these was Mead's friend, Edward Sapir, who began to question just what 'culture' is. Is it like some kind of mould into which individuals are poured or is it the sum of patterned experience? Margaret Mead's career began very much under the tutelage of conventional views, but her accumulated experience (including that of her husbands) and the thinkers with whom she came into contact led her to question almost every accepted tenet. Her enlarged interests were reflected in her co-operation with Bateson in the recording of customs by photography, her interest in semiotics or the theory of how men communicate by gestures and her ability to relate experiences of childhood to adulthood. Her openness to new ideas caused controversy, such as her espousal of Geoffrey Gorer's theory that swaddling practices provided valuable clues to an understanding of the Russian character. But for Mead the study of behaviour patterns always took precedence over the examination of ontogenetic development.

Her career coincided with the golden age of anthropology in the twenties. However flawed *Coming of Age in Samoa* might be with hindsight, it was an inspired decision to travel to a remote island, an adventure which appealed to a universal longing for the exotic and the romantic. Happily Mead's youthful purple prose matched people's expectations.

Boas was delighted because he realized that she had provided him with material that could be utilized in the important role he saw anthropology playing in the years ahead. In 1928 he published *Anthropology and Modern Life*, in which he suggested that the study of primitive man is only the prelude to a much larger study, providing insights into the nature of society at large.

It was thus that Mead became a self-appointed roving ambassador. Many people accepted her at her own evaluation. She was asked to undertake a book for the Rand Corporation, *Soviet Attitudes Toward Authority*, which was published in 1951. She had never visited the USSR; and while her observations may have been legitimate, the very fact that the study was undertaken for an organization whose conservative bias was well known in a sense undermined the credibility of her findings.

During Mead's lifetime some of her peers felt not only condescending but genuinely angry that solid work in anthropology was overlooked because of the hoopla attached to Margaret Mead. Some felt that if there were less emphasis on 'culture' as an abstraction, more might be learned about people as individuals. Few ventured to make a public issue of it, partly because of the substantial support Mead could muster through the wide network she had established, and also because they were afraid that criticism might bring anthropology itself into disrepute. However, long before her death Mead was aware that serious opposition was being mobilized.

When younger anthropologists in subsequent research found data considerably at variance with that of Mead, her reputation in the anthropology establishment was such that they refrained from seriously questioning her conclusions. *Time* magazine in 1969 declared that she had provided 'solid proof' for her findings in Samoa, even though she had never returned to conduct further field work; yet she visited Manus six times between 1927 and 1975. In the prefaces she wrote for successive editions of *Coming of Age in Samoa* she felt confident enough to describe her early account as 'a precious permanent possession'.

In the early 1970s Samoan students studying at American universities were vociferous in demanding that she revise what she had written as a totally misleading depiction of their culture. Her reply: 'It must remain, as all anthropological works must remain, exactly as it was written, true to what I saw in Samoa and what I was able to convey of what I saw, true to the state of our knowledge of human behaviour as it was in the mid 1920s; true to our hopes and fears for the future of the world.'

One might assume that she never returned to Samoa because she wanted her description of it to remain as frozen in time as the figures on Keats's Grecian urn. Similarly in 1977, when she made a brief visit to Bali, she stubbornly insisted that Bali was exactly as it had been in her day, and brusquely brushed aside all the contradictions raised by a young anthropologist who was actually working there. On the other hand, she asserted that the changes in Manus were total – a situation which would not entail extensive re-examination and comparison with her original data. In early 1965 she called together a meeting to persuade the people of Manus to use name and surname so that they could keep bank accounts and records could be maintained more easily. When she failed to gain unanimous co-operation she was extremely annoyed. After all, in *New Lives for Old* she had announced to the world that Manus was a model of moral and political evolution. Margaret Mead was not one who could easily admit that she was wrong about anything, and certainly least of all about the work on which her reputation had been founded.

In November 1964, en route to Manus, Mead visited the Australian National University where she met Derek Freeman, an anthropologist who had spent many years of field work in Samoa. While crossing the Indian Ocean on his recent return from Europe, Freeman had carefully reread *Coming of Age in Samoa* preparatory to another visit to Samoa. As he turned the pages he made annotations in red ballpoint, placing numerous question marks against sections of the text. On 10 November he and Mead met in his office for a discussion about Samoa. Freeman told her frankly that much of her evidence had been proved erroneous, particularly her denial of forceful rape. Mead appeared dumbfounded. At one point Freeman asked her if it was still her view that all Samoan girls had 'perfect adjustment'. Mead denied that she had ever made such a claim, and was visibly annoyed when Freeman pointed to the actual passage. Mead then flicked through the book and, startled by the number of queries in red ink in the margins, grasped Freeman's Pelican edition which she held firmly in her lap during the rest of the discussion so that he could not refer to it. The following day, in a seminar, in response to questions from Freeman, she snapped, 'You think you know everything!'

When she arrived in Manus early in December her colleague, Ted Schwartz's second wife, now Professor Lola Romanucci-Ross, found her greatly agitated. Mead told her of the conversation in Canberra and that Freeman had found her wrong. Romanucci-Ross, in an effort to reassure her, tried to convince her that her reputation no longer depended on her first book. As always activity was the best antidote for anxiety; and she was again the old dynamo of energy from daybreak until late at night, with a break for an afternoon nap, followed by tea with all the ceremony of English custom.

Knowing that Freeman was going to publish a critique of her writings, Mead wrote to him, ending the letter with the words, 'Anyway, what is important is the work.' They continued their conversation by correspondence until 1978, when in August Freeman offered to send her an early draft of his refutation which was almost ready for publication. He received no reply, and by November Mead was dead. She fought frantically against dying; and it must have been a bitter death knowing that in the near future her work would be scrutinized in a way no one had dared to do during her lifetime.

Freeman has been criticized by Mead's supporters as lacking in gallantry by publishing *Margaret Mead in Samoa: The Making and Unmaking of an Anthropological Myth* (1983) so soon after her death. Freeman's explanation for the date of publication of his book is that he was not able to gain access to American Samoan crime records until 1981. He has also been attacked as an unpleasant man who has devoted a lifetime to exposing not only Mead but the entire anthropological establishment which, in his view, had been taken in by her. As he pointed out, Mead's mistaken conclusions were repeated in an unbroken succession of anthropological textbooks. Could it not be plausibly argued that Freeman was extremely brave – more brave, in fact, than those who had been on the scene and had not carried their findings to their logical conclusions? By bringing out his book so soon after Mead's death, it was inevitable that he would also encounter an additional dimension of sentimental protectiveness.

When Freeman first arrived in Samoa in 1940 he was still under the sway of cultural determinism. Within two years he found that the facts coming before his eyes were undeniably forcing him to look at this society differently from the way Mead had done. By then he had learned the language, had been adopted by a Samoan family, and had been granted the honour of sitting on a council of chiefs. Mead, a gullible innocent, had practically no background knowledge of the culture she had come to study. With an inadequate command of Samoan, she acquired her data through information provided by uneducated girls. She never established access to male groups, and, according to Freeman, was taken in by polite manners.

Committed to Boas's side in the fierce nurture-nature debate, Mead's greatest misdemeanour in Freeman's eyes was not simply gullibility, but deliberately setting out to impose her mentor's ideology on the evidence. Freeman describes her attitude as that which T. H. Huxley once called 'the championship of a foregone conclusion'. In Mead's Samoa life was delightfully casual, and in the absence of nuclear families free love was permitted among adolescents and guilt was unknown. Freeman set about demolishing this idyllic image point by point. He found Samoans competitive and touchy, given to violence and jealousy. Mead had reported that 'the idea of forcible rape . . . is completely foreign to the Samoan mind', whereas Freeman found that the incidence of rape was among the highest in the world and all that Mead needed to do to learn this was to glance at the Samoa *Times* while she was there.

Mead herself said that it was 'crazy' that on her first field trip she had stumbled on a culture that fitted Boas's ideas so neatly. Crazy like a fox, said Freeman. He found it more than a curious coincidence that so many of Boas's protégés had the same experience. Ruth Benedict, for example, in *Patterns of Culture*, categorized Indian cultures as either Dionysian, given to passion and frenzy; or Apollonian, characterized by order and restrained emotion; and one was somewhere in between. Similarly in New Guinea Mead was to find the mild Arapesh, the fierce Mundugumor, and in the middle, the Tchambuli.

Freeman has contended that he has not taken the nature side of the dispute: 'The position I take is that both nature and nurture are always significantly different.' In Samoa he found that infants displayed all the behaviour patterns described by John Bowlby in his theories on attachment, and that, contrary to Mead, distinct family units existed within the wide extended family. In short, Mead had returned to America with superficial observations based on limited data, but armed with a theory that was highly in tune with current fantasies about an ideal utopian society which would banish guilt once the barriers protecting the nuclear family were obliterated. Sexual freedom and permissive education were the panaceas she seemed to offer.

While there had been rumblings about Mead within the anthropological establishment for years, its members closed ranks when one of its sacred cows was attacked openly. The important issues which Freeman had raised were seldom discussed. The debate was petulant and undignified; and too often the counter-attack became an ad hominem issue. Freeman himself was attacked as difficult and obsessional, and it was alleged that his main aim in life was to 'get' Margaret Mead. His writing style was described as 'poor' – no one ever explained in what way. Above everything else, Freeman was considered 'tawdry' to wait until Mead could no longer defend herself.

But was there any convincing defence of Mead? Some commentators claimed that Freeman had not taken sufficiently into consideration the fact that Samoan civilization had changed a great deal since Mead's day. One feeble argument would have it that the high rate of suicide among teenagers was due to the fact that young people found the pressures of home chores and schoolwork intolerable. What this argument left out of account was the uncomfortably high suicide rate in Mead's own day. Among all the attacks on Freeman it is difficult to find a legitimately strong argument. It would appear that in time the scandal will be absorbed, the sort of issue that arises from time to time in the history of ideas. In the meantime within university departments Mead's name is evoked less and less frequently. In the Hall of the Peoples of the Pacific at the American Museum of Natural History, once associated more with Mead's name than with any other, the wording on the placard describing the exhibition indicates Mead's present ambiguous status.

Mead achieved her aim in life: to be famous. She achieved fame early, and she worked strenuously all her life to become more and more famous. She once told Lola Romanucci-Ross, 'You are only *one person away* from anybody in the world you want to get to know, and you know all you have to do is ask me.' In countries like Mexico, Italy, or France, where her younger colleague was fluent in the languages, Mead made it clear that it was her job to let it be known that a great celebrity was in their midst. In a sense there was a real meeting of Mead's narcissistic needs and the narcissistic values of her society. Fame, even more than money, was the highest goal of many Americans.

The supreme irony of Mead's life is the way in which she has achieved posthumous fame. Thousands of young people who have never read Mead's books know her name precisely because interest in her has been rekindled by having her lifetime's work seriously questioned.

*Books by Margaret Mead*

*And Keep Your Powder Dry.* New York: William Morrow, 1975 (orig. publ. 1942).

*Balinese Character: A Photographic Analysis* (with Gregory Bateson). New York: Academy of Sciences, 1962.

*Blackberry Winter: My Earlier Years.* New York : 1972; Pocket Books, 1975.

*Coming of Age in Samoa: A Psychological Study of Primitive Youth for Western Civilization.* New York: William Morrow, 1961 (orig. publ. 1928).

*Growing Up in New Guinea: A Comparative Study of Primitive Education.* New York: William Morrow, 1975 (orig. publ. 1930).

*Letters from the Field 1925–1965.* New York: Harper and Row, 1977.

*Male and Female: A Study of the Sexes in a Changing World.* New York: William Morrow, 1975 (orig. publ. 1960).

*New Lives for Old: Cultural Transformation – Manus 1928–1953.* New York: William Morrow, 1975 (orig. publ. 1960).

*A Rap on Race* (with James Baldwin). Philadelphia and New York: J. B. Lippincott, 1971.

MARGARET MEAD

*Sex and Temperament in Three Primitive Societies.* New York: William Morrow, 1963 (orig. publ. 1935).

*World Enough: Rethinking the Future* (photographs by Ken Heyman). Boston: Little, Brown, 1975.


*Books about Margaret Mead*

These books were invaluable in the preparation of this text:

Bateson, Mary Catherine: *With a Daughter's Eye. A Memoir of Margaret Mead and Gregory Bateson.* New York: William Morrow, 1984.

Freeman, Derek: *Margaret Mead and Samoa: The Making and Unmaking of an Anthropological Myth.* Cambridge, Mass. and London, England: Harvard University Press, 1983.

Howard, Jane: *Margaret Mead: A Life.* New York: Simon and Schuster, 1984.

I wish to thank Dr Ronald S. Wilkinson and his staff in the Manuscript Division, Library of Congress, for their courteous help in allowing me to examine the Mead papers.

P.G.